The Experience of No-Self

Also by Bernadette Roberts:

The Path to No-Self

What is Self?

Spiritual Journey Recapitulates the History of Religion

THE EXPERIENCE OF NO-SELF

A Contemplative Journey

Bernadette Roberts

State University of New York Press

Published by
State University of New York Press, Albany

© 1993 by Bernadette Roberts

Printed in the United States of America

For information, address State University of New York Press,
State University Plaza, Albany, N.Y., 12246

Production by Marilyn P. Semerad
Marketing by Theresa A. Swierzowski

Library of Congress Cataloging-in-Publication Data
Roberts, Bernadette, 1931-
    The experience of no-self : a contemplative journey /
Bernadette Roberts. — Rev. ed.
        p. cm.
    ISBN 0-7914-1694-1 (pbk. : alk. paper)
    1. Contemplation—Case studies. 2. Depersonalization—
Religious aspects—Christianity—Case studies. 3. Roberts,
Bernadette, 1931-. 4. Catholics—United States—Biography.
I. Title.
BV5091.C7R6 1992
248.2'2'092—dc20
[B]   92-47401
                                                              CIP

10   9

*To contemplatives East and West—especial-
ly those who dwell on the spiritual mountains of Carmel and New Camaldoli*

Contents

Introduction

This is the personal account of a two-year journey during which I experienced the falling away of everything I can call a self. It was a journey through an unknown passageway that led to a life so new and different that, despite forty years of varied contemplative experiences, I never suspected its existence. Because it was beyond my expectations, the experience of no-self remained incomprehensible in terms of any frame of reference known to me, and though I searched the libraries and bookstores I did not find there an explanation or an account of a similar journey which, at the time, would have been clarifying and most helpful. Owing then to the deficiency of recorded accounts, I have written these pages trusting that they may be of use to those who share the destiny of making this journey beyond the self.

Though my contemplative experiences began at an early age, it was not until I was fifteen that I discovered how these experiences fit like the inset of a child's puzzle into the larger framework of the Christian contemplative tradition. This finding was followed by ten years of relative seclusion in order to pursue the Christian goal of union with God, and once I had the certitude of this goal's realization, I entered the more ordinary stream of life where I remain to this day.

Within the traditional framework, the Christian notion of loss-of-self is generally regarded as the transformation or loss of the ego (lower self) as it attains to the higher or true self in its union with God. In this union, however, self retains its individual uniqueness and never loses its ontological sense of personal self-hood. Thus being lost to myself meant, at the same time, being found in God as the sharer of a divine life. From here on, the deepest sense of being and life is equally the sense of God's being and life. Thus there is no longer any sense of "my" life, but rather "our" life—God and self. In this abiding state God, the "still-point" at the center of being, is ever accessible to the contemplative gaze—a point from which the life of self arises and into which it sometimes disappears. But this latter experience of loss-of-self is only transient, it does not constitute a permanent state, nor did it occur to me that it could ever do so in this life.

Prior to this present journey, I had given little thought to the self, its perimeters or definitions. I took for granted the self was the totality of being, body and soul, mind and feelings; a being centered in God, its power-axis and still-point. Thus, because self at its deepest center is a run-on with the divine, I never found any true self apart from God, for to find the One is to find the other.

Because this was the limit of my expectations, I was all the more surprised and bewildered when many years later I came upon a permanent state in which there was no self, no higher self, true self, or anything that could be called a self. Clearly, I had fallen outside my own, as well as the traditional frame of reference, when I came upon a path that seemed to begin where the writers on the contemplative life had left off. But with the clear certitude of the self's disappearance, there automatically arose the question of what had fallen away— what was the self? What, exactly, had it been? Then too, there was the all-important question: what remained in its absence? This journey was the gradual revelation of the answers to these questions, answers that had to be derived solely from personal experience since no outside explanation was forthcoming.

With the exception of the little I could find by Meister Eckhart, I was left without a way to account for this experience, and even when I turned to books in the Eastern traditions, I encountered the same deficit of accounts—at least accounts that were available to me through the local channels. Though the Buddhist notion of no-self struck me as true, its failure to acknowledge, or first come upon the wholeness of the self in its union with God, naturally left the Christian experience of no-self unaccounted for. Quite possibly, the extent to which the individual first discovers this union is the extent to which its falling away will appear all the more inexplicable and bewildering. It is only when this transition is over, or when we have become acclimated to a new life, that the relative difference between self and no-self recedes beyond reach; but by this time, we have already seen what is down the road and the need for clarification no longer exists.

Realizing then, that I was alone in this gap between the ultimate Christian notion of loss-of-self and its immediate experience, I came to a few conclusions of my own. In main, I am convinced that the contemplative life is composed of two distinct and separate movements well marked and defined by the nature of their experiences alone. The first movement is toward self's union with God which seems to run parallel with the psychological process of integration, wherein the emphasis is on interior trials and dark nights by which the self is established in a permanent union with God, the still-point and axis of its being. In this process we discover that self is not lost; rather, a new self is revealed that functions from the deepest, innermost divine center.

Following this first movement is an interval (twenty years in my case) during which this union is tested by a variety of exterior (not interior) trials whereby this oneness is revealed in all its enduring depths of stability and toughness against all forces that would move, fragment, or disturb its center. Thus it is a period of discovering the beauty and intense wonder of this gratuitous union and, above all, of discovering what this wholeness means and how it works in our daily lives in the marketplace. Initially it is a period of becoming acclimated to the relative difference between life with the old, easily fragmented self, and life with a new self that cannot be moved from its center in God. Finally, this is a stage in which, if exterior trials are not forthcoming, the contemplative may seek them because the energy created by this union must move outward (as a unit and not as a scattered force) to find expression, to accept challenge—even suffering—as a way to both reveal and affirm this enduring love.

I might add that these intervening years between movements are also largely ignored in contemplative literature; their importance is highly underestimated due to the failure to realize that this interval (the "marketplace stage") is actually the preparation for a great explosion—a quiet one, however—that ushers in another major turning-point. It seems that at the end of the marketplace a point is reached where the self is so completely aligned with the still-point that it can no longer be moved, even in its first movements, from this center. It can no longer be tested by any force or trial, nor moved by the winds of change, and at this point the self has obviously outworn its function; it is no longer needed or useful, and life can go on without it. We are ready to move on, to go beyond the self, beyond even its most intimate union with God, and this is where we enter yet another new life—a life best categorized, perhaps, as a life without a self.

The onset of this second movement is characterized by the falling away of self and coming upon "that" which remains when it is gone. But this going-out is an upheaval, a complete turnabout of such proportions it cannot possibly be missed, under-emphasized, or sufficiently stressed as a major landmark in the contemplative life. It is far more than the discovery of life without a self. The immediate, inevitable result is an emergence into a new dimension of knowing and being that entails a difficult and prolonged readjustment. The reflexive mechanism of the mind—or whatever it is that allows us to be self-conscious—is cut off or permanently suspended so the mind is ever after held in a fixed now-moment out of which it cannot move in its uninterrupted gaze upon the Unknown.

This journey then, is nothing more, yet nothing less than a period of acclimating to a new way of seeing, a time of transition and revelation as it gradually comes upon "that" which remains when there is no self. This is not a journey for those who expect love and bliss, rather, it is for the hardy who have been tried in fire and have come to rest in a tough, immovable trust in "that" which lies beyond the known, beyond the self, beyond union, and even beyond love and trust itself.

Since the moment self-consciousness comes to a permanent end—and a new journey begins—is such a decisive stroke or milestone in the contemplative life, I can only speculate why so little has been said of this breakthrough; in fact, I may never get over the silence on the part of writers who say nothing about this second movement. Perhaps some contemplatives take in stride what to others is a monumental explosion; or possibly, writers down-play what they do not understand or deem unorthodox or rare; or perhaps—and this is my view—they have confused these two movements by failing to adequately distinguish between them: that is, to distinguish between a radical *change* of consciousness and the *cessation* of consciousness; between going beyond first, the lower (ego) self, and later, the higher True Self; between union with God, and God beyond union. Since viewed as a whole, the contemplative life is on a single continuum, it is often difficult to draw a line and see clear distinctions until one has personally encountered these landmarks, at which time the difference between these movements becomes obvious and unmistakable.

My purpose then, in writing this account, is to help clarify the second movement, to make it more recognizable and to bring to light, if possible, the ultimate, final realization of the Christian notion of loss-of-self. In part, this attempt stems from the conviction that this movement is not unusual and that many individuals have come, or will come, to this stage wherein some clarification will be as relevant to them as it would have been to me. Though no two will have the same experiences, I feel sure that for those who had found their true self in God and then lost it, there will be certain consequences and findings in common.

While the journey was in progress, I tried to write of its events, but it was not until it was over—or until the relative difference between life with or without a self was no longer apparent—that I wrote the account in its present form and gave it to several friends for their comments and criticisms. Though much too generous to cite me for either its content or its homely narrative, they were nevertheless honest with their questions and objections. In response to these I wrote Part II, trying to find the answers that were not apparent during the transition.

In some respects, while writing these final chapters I learned more about the journey than I learned while it was in progress. It seems that the nature of this passage is a total state of unknowing which, while it lent a certain beauty and air of mystery to its unfoldment, also lent a sense of bewilderment which was responsible, I believe, for certain hardships that might have been avoided if some explanation had been forthcoming. It was only when the journey was over and I could view it in retrospect that I came to a better understanding, and was able, therefore, to offer the explanations given in the final chapters.

Here too, I have made reference to my earlier background where it seemed necessary for understanding the present journey in its relationship to the past.

This background was not given at the outset because my present concern focuses solely on that relatively unexplored dimension of life—the movement beyond self. Also, I knew that if I did not record this transition as soon as possible it would soon be forgotten, because one of the first lessons learned on this journey is that the passing of each experience leaves nothing in its wake, hardly a footprint, and certainly not a vivid memory. In a word, one learns to live without a past.

For this reason I wrote quickly before the journey became lost forever and life without a self grew as dim as the day of my birth. But at the same time, release from the past has made it possible to write on a personal level—something I would not have dared to undertake prior to this time—because the journey no longer belongs to "me." I look upon it as I do any other fact of life or event taking place around us. Thus it now stands unalterably by itself where it remains forever—but a thing of the past.

In conclusion, I must re-emphasize that the following experiences do not belong to the first contemplative movement or the soul's establishment in a state of union with God. I have written elsewhere of this first journey and feel that enough has been said of it already, since this movement is inevitably the exclusive concern of contemplative writers. Thus it is only where these writers leave off that I propose to begin. Here now, begins the journey beyond union, beyond self and God, a journey into the silent and still regions of the Unknown.

Part I

The Journey

Chapter 1

Through past experience I had become familiar with many different types and levels of silence. There is a silence within, a silence that descends from without; a silence that stills existence and a silence that engulfs the entire universe. There is a silence of the self and its faculties of will, thought, memory, and emotions. There is a silence in which there is nothing, a silence in which there is something; and finally, there is the silence of noself and the silence of God. If there was any path on which I could chart my contemplative experiences, it would be this ever-expanding and deepening path of silence.

On one occasion, however, this path seemed to come to an end when I entered a silence from which I would never totally emerge. But I must preface this account by saying that on previous occasions, I had come upon a pervasive silence of the faculties so total as to give rise to subtle apprehensions of fear. It was a fear of being engulfed forever, of being lost, annihilated, or blacking out and possibly never returning. In such moments, to ward off the fear, I would make some movement of abandoning my fate to God—a gesture of the will, a thought, some type of projection. And every time

I did this the silence would be broken and I would gradually return to my usual self—and security. Then, one day, this was not to be the case.

Down the road from where I lived there was a monastery by the sea, and on afternoons when I could get away I liked to spend some time alone in the silence of its chapel. This particular afternoon was no different than others. Once again there was a pervasive silence and once again I waited for the onset of fear to break it up. But this time the fear never came. Whether by habit of expectation or the reality of a fear held in abeyance, I felt some moments of suspense or tension—as if waiting for fear to touch me. During these moments of waiting I felt as if I were poised on a precipice or balanced on a thin tightrope, with the known (myself) on one side and the unknown (God) on the other. A movement of fear would have been a movement toward the self and the known. Would I pass over this time, or would I fall back into my self—as usual? Since there was no power of my own to move or choose I knew the decision was not mine; within, all was still, silent and motionless. In this stillness I was not aware of the moment when the fear and tension of waiting had left. Still, I continued to wait for a movement not of myself and when no movement came, I simply remained in a great stillness.

Sister was rattling the keys of the chapel door. It was time to lock up, and time to go home and prepare dinner for my children. Always in the past, having to abruptly pull out of a deep silence was difficult, for my energies were then at a low ebb, and the effort of moving was like lifting a dead weight. This time, however, it suddenly occurred to me not to think about getting up, but to just *do* it. I think I learned a valuable lesson here, because I left the chapel as a feather floats in the wind. Once outside, I fully expected to return to my ordinary energies and thinking mind, but this day I had a difficult time because I was continually falling back into the great silence. The drive home was a constant battle against complete unconsciousness, and trying to get dinner was like trying to move a mountain.

For three exhausting days it was a battle to stay awake and ward off the silence that every second threatened to overpower me. The only way I could accomplish the minimum of chores was by persistently reminding myself of what I was doing: now I'm peeling the carrots, now I'm cutting them, now I'm getting out a pan, now I'm putting water in the pan and on and on until, finally, I was so exhausted I would have to run for the couch. The moment I lay down I immediately blacked out. Sometimes it seemed I was out for hours, when it was only five minutes; at other times, it seemed like five minutes when it was hours. In this blackout there were no dreams, no awareness of my surroundings, no thoughts, no experiences—absolutely nothing.

On the fourth day I noticed the silence easing up so I could stay awake with less effort and, therefore, trusted myself to go shopping for groceries. I do not know what happened, but suddenly a lady was shaking me and asking, "Are you asleep?" I smiled at her while trying to get my bearings because, for the moment, I had not the slightest idea how I got in the store or what I should be doing. So I had to start all over again: now I am pushing the basket, now I must get some oranges, and so on. The morning of the fifth day, I could not find my slippers anywhere, but when getting breakfast for the children I opened the refrigerator and what I found there was unbelievable, positively ludicrous.

By the ninth day, the silence had so eased up I felt assured that a little while longer and all would be normal again. But as the days went by and I was once more able to function as usual I noticed something was missing, but I couldn't put my finger on it. Something, or some part of me had not returned. Some part of me was still in silence. It was as if some part of my mind had closed down. I blamed it on the memory because it was the last to return, and when it finally did, I noticed how flat and lifeless it was—like colorless slides on an antique film. It was dead. Not only was the distant past empty, but also the past of the previous minutes.

Now when something is dead you soon lose the habit of trying to resurrect it; thus when the memory is lifeless you learn to live as one who has no past—you learn to live in the present moment. That this could now be done effortlessly—and out of sheer necessity—was one good outcome of an otherwise exhausting experience. And even when I regained my practical memory, the effortless living in the present never left. But with the return of a practical memory I discounted my earlier notion of what was missing and decided that the silent aspect of my mind was actually a kind of "absorption," an absorption in the unknown, which for me, of course, was God. It was like a continuous gaze at the great, silent Unknowable which no activity could interrupt. This was another welcomed outcome of the initial experience.

This interpretation of the silent aspect of my mind (absorption) seemed sufficiently explanatory for about a month when I again changed my mind and decided that this absorption was actually an awareness, a special kind of "seeing" so that what had really happened was not a close-down of any kind, but actually an opening-up; nothing was missing, "something" had been added. After a while, however, this notion also did not seem to fit, it was somehow dissatisfying, something else had happened. So I decided to go to the library to see if I could solve this mystery through someone else's experience.

What I found out is that, if it cannot be found in the works of John of the Cross, it will probably not be found at all. While the writings of the Saint were well known to me, I could not find there an explanation of my specific experience; nor was I able to find it anywhere in the library. But coming home that day, walking downhill with a panorama of valley and hills before me, I turned my gaze inward, and what I saw, stopped me in my tracks. Instead of the usual unlocalized center of myself, there was nothing there, it was empty; and at the moment of seeing this there was a flood of quiet joy and I knew, finally I knew what was missing—it was my "self."

Physically I felt as if a great burden had been lifted from me, I felt so light I looked down at my feet to be sure they were on the ground. Later I thought of St. Paul's experience, "Now, not I, but Christ lives in me," and realized that despite my emptiness no one else had moved in to take my place. So I decided that Christ WAS the joy, the emptiness itself; He was all that was left of this human experience. For days I walked with this joy that, at times, was so great, I marveled at the flood gates and wondered how long they would hold.

This experience was the height of my contemplative vocation. It was the ending of a question that had plagued me for years: where do "I" leave off and God begin? Over the years the line that separated us had grown so thin and faded that most of the time I couldn't see it at all, but always my mind had wanted desperately to know: what was His and what was mine? Now my quandary was over. There was no "mine" anymore, there was only His. I could have lived in this joyous state the rest of my life, but such was not in the Great Plan. It was just a matter of days, a week perhaps, when my entire spiritual life—the work, the suffering, the experiences and the goals of a lifetime—suddenly exploded into a million irretrievable pieces and there was nothing, absolutely nothing left.

Chapter 2

When the joy of my own emptiness began to wane I decided to rejuvenate it by spending some solitary time gazing into my empty self. Though the center of self was gone, I was sure the remaining emptiness, the silence and joy, was God Himself. Thus on one occasion, with full hedonistic deliberation, I settled myself down and turned my gaze inward. Almost immediately the empty space began to expand, and expanded so rapidly it seemed to explode; then, in the pit of my stomach I had the feeling of falling a hundred floors in a nonstop elevator, and in this fall every sense of life was drained from me. The moment of landing I knew: *When there is no personal self, there is also no personal God.* I saw clearly how the two go together—and where they went, I have never found out.

For a while I sat there mentally and emotionally stunned. I couldn't think about what had happened, nor was there any response in me at all. Around me there was only stillness, and in this complete stillness I waited and waited for some kind of reaction to set in or something to happen next, but nothing ever did. In me there was no sense of life, no movement and no feeling; finally I realized I no longer had a "within" at all.

The moment of falling had been such a complete wipe-out that never again would I have any sense of possessing a life I could call my own—or any other type of life. My interior or spiritual life was finished. There was no more gazing within; from now on my eyes could only look outward. At the time, I had no way of knowing the tremendous repercussions that would follow this sudden event. I had to learn bit by bit on a totally experiential level. My mind could not comprehend what had happened; this event and everything that followed fell outside any frame of reference known to me. From here on, I literally had to grope my way along an unknown path.

My first thought was: oh, no, not another Dark Night! I was accustomed to those experiential disappearances of God and was rather disappointed to think there were any of them left. But when none of the usual reactions set in (anything from anxiety to agony—you name it), I felt this experience fell outside anything John of the Cross had described and put the notion out of my mind. Besides, it didn't make any difference, I simply had to cope with the reality of the here and now, a reality in which there was no sense of life in me.

So I sat there fully awake, healthy, faculties unimpaired, obviously alive; in a word, all systems were functioning as usual—but I felt no life. What do you do now? I decided I might as well get an early start preparing dinner, but as I did so, all the usual movements now seemed so mechanical I felt I had suddenly become a robot, for I could no longer endow my work with any personal energies. I did my chores with no life to back them up and they were all totally mechanical, a mere conditioned habit of movement.

After a while this "gets" to you and you gradually have a pressing need to find some life somewhere. Hoping to find it I went into the garden and stood there looking around. I knew there was life there, but I couldn't "feel" it; so I went around like a blind man, touching everything: the leaves and flowers; reaching up I grabbed the pine branches and let them slide through my hands; stooping down, I ran my hands through the soil. Then I lay down on the grass, palms downward, looking up through the branches of the pine tree and felt the moving air flow over me. It was good to be there; everything was okay. Somewhere there was life all around me, even if there was no life in me.

Later that evening before the sun went down I took myself to a place I always went in time of crisis— the local bird refuge. It was only a few blocks from home and the route there passed by beautiful vistas of the sea, with its miles of shoreline and hills rising up behind the refuge. Usually I only climbed in a little way, for beyond the stump where I would sit was a marsh that grew deeper with mud and water as it approached one of the ponds formed by the river which here, emptied into the sea. But this day I took off my shoes and socks and climbed into the middle of the refuge until I found a small rock barely visible above the mud. Here, among the tall reeds and wild grasses I sat down and disappeared—literally sank into the life that was around me, and soon, on me as well.

Always I had felt at home here. It was a place of great peace and a mysterious stillness. By experience I knew that thinking would never solve the problems of life, it was just being here, out-of-doors, in the midst of real life, that automatically separated the relevant from the irrelevant, so that upon returning home all the irrelevancies had been swept away and I could see clearly the path I must go. So too, on this particular day I knew I was home, more at home perhaps than ever before. Around the little rock life was teeming and overflowing; it was everywhere, and so compensated for my own lack of life that the earlier events of the day seemed not to have happened. For sure, this was where I belonged, surrounded and locked securely into this elusive unlocalized thing called "life." After all, I thought, perhaps no man is better than the elements of which he is composed, for these elements are his very life—but how this could be so, I did not know. Just to be there was all that mattered.

The next weeks were spent mainly out-of-doors. Life indoors had become almost intolerable because it was now so routine, lifeless, and devoid of personal energies that it was all I could do to accomplish the minimum of chores. But out-of-doors somewhere life was flowing—peaceful, forgetful, unknowable—and this was where I had to be. So I roamed the hills, the riverbanks and the seashore just looking, watching, and being there.

Though I had looked and watched all my life, this time was different because I could no more find life in the trees, the wild flowers or the waters than I could find it in myself; and yet, there was life all around. It's strange how the mind wants to localize and pinpoint this unknowable thing called life, and when its demands are met, it goes blind with this knowledge and is forever locked out of the only true security man has—or so I would soon learn. For now, however, I was looking for this security and could not find it. Though everything seemed as empty as myself I knew there was life somewhere in nature, and for now, I wanted only to be there and be a part of it.

On a bluff above the sea, overlooking a cove of rocks on which the seals would doze, there stood a gnarled, wind-blown cypress tree, a favorite spot of mine—until a Forest Ranger one day told me to leave, lest I add to the soil erosion. Between the tortured roots, which allowed for no other growth, there was a place to sit down without mashing a single dandelion or disturbing the varied flora that made this bluff so beautiful.

It was here that nature finally yielded its secret to me in a simple, still moment in which I saw how it all worked. God or life was not *in* anything, it was just the reverse: everything was *in* God. And we were not *in* God like drops of water that could be separated from the sea, but more like . . . well, the only thing I could think of was the notion of trying to pinch out a spot on an inflated balloon; if you pinch out a spot and try to cut it off the whole thing will pop because it can't be done. You cannot separate anything from God, for as soon as you let go of the notion of separateness, everything falls back into the wholeness of God and life.

But to see how this works and to explain it are two different matters. One thing is for sure: as long as we are caught up in words, definitions, and all that the mind wants to cling to, we can never see how it works. And until we can go beyond our notions regarding the true nature of life we will never realize how totally secure we really are, and how all the fighting for individual survival and self-security is a waste of energy. This insight then, opened a new door for me. I began to see things differently and, above all, I quit wandering around looking for life—obviously it's everywhere, we're in it; it's all there is.

Solely in retrospect I would like to mention a certain lesson learned on this journey. I learned that a single insight is not sufficient to bring about any real change. In time, every insight has a way of filtering down to our usual frame of reference, and once we make it fit, it gets lost in the milieu of the mind—the mind, which has a tendency to pollute every insight. The secret of allowing an insight to become a permanent way of knowing and seeing is not to touch it, cling to it, dogmatize it, or even think about it. Insights come and go, but to have them stay we have to flow with them, otherwise no change is possible. It is a mistake to think that because we have been thrown the ball, we know which direction to run. Perhaps our greatest insights are lost this way: we plunk them down in our usual frame of reference and go nowhere. But if we are really ready when the ball comes, the sheer momentum will carry us and place us in the flow—wherever it is going. Now I pass this along only because I had to learn it the hard way. When the pieces didn't fit or when an insight fell outside my frame of reference I felt more lost than was really necessary. Thus I could have saved myself a lot of trouble looking and searching for my own unanswerable questions.

An example of learning the hard way occurred here, with the falling away of all feeling of possessing individual life, which forced me to look for life outside myself. Since I had already lived some forty years experiencing life within, this was a very difficult time, a time of transition and acclimation without being able to see ahead or understanding what had happened. Nevertheless, I did the best I could to help myself, and since I was a daily communicant, it occurred to me it might be of some avail to carry the Eucharist with me at all times—in a pix around my neck. With the falling away of life within, the reception of the Eucharist no longer had any effect on me. Where before it had always drawn me into its mysterious silence, now, no such change occurred. If anything, there was too much silence. Thus, with the failure of the Eucharist to restore a sense of life within, I felt doubly lost and decided I might at least carry it with me in my search to find God without.

After a few weeks, however, I saw this ruse was not working when it brought no sense of life or security, nor brought about any change in the situation. Then, under the cypress tree on the day already mentioned, I consumed the host and saw all things were in God, that he was closer and more personal than I ever dared to expect. To suddenly realize you live and walk in God is a unique discovery that forever dispels the sense of loss that ensues when the feeling of a personal life falls away.

If nothing else, this incident (and many that remain untold) attests to my continual effort to cling to the usual frame of reference, a clinging that revealed nothing until the hold was released. I might add that among the many notions that had to be abandoned was my notion of abandonment itself. It was not I, who had abandoned the self to God, rather it was God who had abandoned the self completely; and once beyond the self, everything goes, even "that" which I had expected would remain.

A week or two after the above insight, I was making a retreat with the Hermit Monks on the Big Sur. About the second day, toward late afternoon, I was standing on their windy hillside looking down over the ocean when a seagull came into view, gliding, dipping, playing with the wind. I watched it as I had never watched anything before in my life. I almost seemed to be mesmerized; it was as if I was watching myself flying, for there was not the usual division between us. Yet something more was there than just a lack of separateness, "something" truly beautiful and unknowable. Finally I turned my eyes to the pine-covered hills behind the monastery and still, there was no division, only something "there" that was flowing with and through every vista and particular object of vision. To see the Oneness of everything is like having special 3D glasses put before your eyes; I thought to myself: for sure, this is what they mean when they say "God IS Everywhere."

I could have stood there looking for the rest of my life, but after a while I thought it was all too good to be true; it was some hoax of the mind and when the bell rang, it would all disappear. Well, the bell finally rang, and it rang the next day and for the rest of the week, but the 3D glasses were still intact. What I had taken as a trick of the mind was to become a permanent way of seeing and knowing which I will do my best to describe as my whole world turned slowly inside-out. I was never to revert back to the usual relative way of seeing separateness or individuality; but make no mistake, the obliteration of separateness is meaningless in itself. What is important about this way of seeing is THAT into which all separateness dissolves.

Before going further and attempting to describe this new way of seeing, I would like to say that after discovering God Everywhere—or His Oneness, as I called it—I was compensated a thousandfold for the bewildering loss of a personal God within. It seems I had first to move through the personal and then the impersonal before I realized God was closer than either and beyond them both.

The notions and the experiences of God as being personally within or impersonally without are purely relative experiences, pertaining to the self and its particular type of consciousness. God, however, is beyond the relativity of our minds and experiences; indeed, he is so close he can never be localized. But to realize this closeness—to see it—is to discover that the very definition of God is "Everywhere." Thus God IS Everywhere and all that truly exists, because wherever we look there is nothing else to see. In truth then, God is neither personal nor impersonal, neither within nor without, but everywhere in general and nowhere in particular. Simply put: God is all that truly exists—all, of course, but the self.

Chapter 3

Eventually it became imperative to make some changes in my life-style. For the time being at least, it had become impossible to feel at one with the constant flow of irrelevancies and noise that made up my usual environment. Having been robbed of the energies necessary to dominate, control, and stay on top of the frequent chaotic conditions in the home, my effectiveness as a mother to four teenagers dropped sharply to zero. When self is no longer running the show, the usual defense-mechanisms can no longer be activated and the burden of coping falls squarely upon the energies of the physical body alone. While I never had the feeling of being nervous, upset, anxious and all that, I nevertheless had the impression that if I were to continue the same pattern of living I would be expected, from now on, to lift dead weights, and I couldn't do it.

Until the rug (my "self") had been pulled out from under me, I never realized how utterly dependent I was upon getting around under my own steam—steam of the mind and emotions, that is—not physical steam. It seems we possess an endless array of subtle energies we don't know we have until they are gone—although later I was to see clearly how these energies are, in fact, the self's defenses against its own annihilation. For right now, however, it was taking a long time to learn how to survive without the experience of any energy. Learning to live this way was like learning to live all over again, and though I now understand it in retrospect, at the time I was as bewildered and groping as a man who has suddenly lost the power of his limbs.

What I seemed to need were great blocks of time for uninterrupted silence and contact with nature, because it was only in such a milieu that I felt at home and at one with the flow of life. What I eventually did was pack up the camping gear and head for the forests of the high Sierras where I camped for five months, or until the snows came and I had to come down.

I went to the mountains to learn how to live a new type of existence, an existence without time, without thought, without the emotions, feelings, and energies of self. I hadn't the slightest idea how things would go; all I knew was that I had to go and find out. While the discoveries were numerous and I have much to say about this adventure, I think I can sum it up in one phrase by saying: until I went to the mountains I had never truly lived. Not for a single day in my life had I ever lived before. Without a doubt I was in the Great Flow, so totally at one with it that every notion of ecstasy, bliss, love and joy, pale by comparison to the extraordinary simplicity, clarity, and oneness of such an existence.

There is nothing haphazard, idle, or easy-going about forest life. On the contrary, everything there is vital, fully awake, dynamic, and intelligent. It is not a free life. The Great Flow takes its own direction, sweeping everything along, and whether it would go or not, is of no consequence. There is no time to step out of the flow or to take a break; in a word, it is a life completely devoid of a single irrelevancy.

One of the great mysteries I hoped to solve in this mountain solitude was the answer to my question: what is it that sees this Oneness everywhere? And to make the question more understandable, I am going to back up a bit to the weeks following the initial seeing on the monks' hillside.

Gradually I began to notice a shift in this seeing. Where at first it had been nebulous and general, I soon noticed that when I visually focused in on a flower, an animal, another person, or any particular object, slowly the particularity would recede into a nebulous Oneness, so that the object's distinctness was lost to my mind. Visually of course, nothing changed, the change was merely in the type of perception itself. Until this happened, it never occurred to me how I had always taken for granted the individuality of all objects of visual perception. But now, with the imposition of the 3D glasses, it became impossible for the mind to perceive or retain any individuality when all visual objects either faded from the mind, gave way to something else, or were "seen through"—I do not know which is the best description to use. I might also add, I do not understand the mechanism of this change in perception, yet I regard this change as one of the most significant events in the entire journey. It not only remained as a permanent irreversible fixture of perception, but it seemed to be the necessary vehicle by which I eventually came to the final "seeing."

It is truly marvelous how this works, it is a unique type of experience; but I repeat, the marvel of it isn't the loss of individuality of the object observed; rather, the marvel is *that* into which it blends and ultimately disappears. For now I called *that* "Oneness"—and of course, "God."

I am always reluctant to use the word "God," because everybody seems to carry around their own stagnant images and definitions that totally cloud the ability to step outside a narrow, individual frame of reference. If we have any conception of what God is, certainly it should be changing and expanding as we ourselves grow and change. This is the very nature of our life's movement: to expand, to open up and blossom. Like flowers that will turn completely backward to face the light, sometimes we too must do an about-face if we would see what IS. Since we do not know in which direction to turn, we must wait like the flower for the morning sun, and with no effort or resistance, be pulled in the direction of the light. Whatever we care to call the ultimate reality, we cannot define or qualify it because the brain is incapable of processing this kind of data. Thus we must ever look upon words as mere descriptions of man's experiences—the nature of which we do not really know. For myself, the opening up of everything upon which I gazed revealed a reality that was the same throughout, be the object animate or inanimate. For this reason I called it, Oneness. That someone else would prefer a different name is all right with me. Just the seeing of IT is all that matters.

The mysterious aspect of this type of seeing was that while I could focus on the objects around me, I could never focus on myself. To do so would have been as impossible as looking into my eyes without a mirror. For this reason I felt like an outside observer looking upon a Oneness that included everything but myself. It was as if I was not a part of this Oneness, not even a part of the universe; in fact, I couldn't see where I had any existence at all. Besides the body, all that was left was just this seeing and yet, even this did not really belong to me for it was not localized anywhere in my mental or physical make-up, but instead, seemed to be on top or a little above my head—toward the front and over the forehead. Although I continued to refer to this seeing as my wonderful glasses—because of the extra dimensional aspect—I was sure this seeing was actually outside the ordinary mind and physical body as well.

While trying to figure out the nature of this seeing, I came upon the notion of man's original consciousness, or the type of consciousness we all have from the beginning. As a one-time student of child development, I knew that the infant possesses a non-relative consciousness in which there is no distinguishing between subject (himself) and object; consequently, he has no notion of a self. Furthermore, as we all know, the infant doesn't think, for as yet there is no content in his consciousness, nor does he have anything to remember. All of us then, were born without a reflective, self-conscious type of mind which, to me, is an apt definition of "seeing." Thus for the adult, seeing may be a kind of return to this original form of consciousness, a form that surprisingly does not seem to hamper the ordinary activities of practical living. Therefore, in the process of reverting back to our original consciousness we have to learn how to live without any self-consciousness—the build-up of a lifetime perhaps—which is not an easy adjustment to make. But it's exciting to think we can make it at all, and even more exciting to think of what would happen if every man could live as he was originally intended to live.

For a while then, this idea of man's original consciousness seemed to clarify the nature of this seeing, but one day I discovered a hole in this conclusion. While there may be no self-consciousness in this seeing, the seeing alone constitutes some form of subject, just as the Oneness it sees, constitutes an object, for the distinction between the seeing and the Oneness was clear to me and never lent itself to any form of identity. In this case, then, seeing (observing) is not identical with the seen (observed), which put me right back on a purely relative plane of existence—even though there is no self that does the seeing. What this means is that the infant's consciousness may actually be relative even though it is not self-reflecting. But however this works, I could never find any relationship between this seeing and Oneness because, as I have said, at all times they were totally distinct and separate.

Months later, this same question of relationship came up in a conversation, and while trying to think of an answer, the notions of original consciousness, seeing, and Oneness, seemed to float out the window and over the hillside until they finally disappeared from sight somewhere over the ocean. Thus the question of relationship of seer and seen had no answer. But at the time of which I speak, I was still thinking up the questions because I lived a full nine months with the wonderful glasses ever focused on the Oneness they saw everywhere, and as far as I was concerned, this was the end of the road.

Nevertheless, it is still interesting to speculate about what the infant may actually see and know before his mind has become conditioned. At the same time we may ponder the animal's type of knowing and the possibility that it may know and see something that man has lost in his endless battle for survival of his self. Then too, who knows what great intelligence may be locked into the very elements that compose man and the universe—an intelligence without any consciousness at all? One thing is certain: with our thinking, rational mind, we'll never come upon these answers because our mind, limited tool that it is, is so continually taken up in the service of self that it cannot come upon that which lies beyond all such concerns.

Apart from trying to identify what it was that saw this Oneness, there was still the unresolved question of what remained in the absence of self. What is this that walks and talks and is aware of the eye upon Oneness? As obvious as it was, I had no mind for such a mystery and could not come upon any satisfying explanation. Though the identity of the Oneness was known, the identity of the eye that saw it, as well as what remained in the absence of self, could not be identified. Thus between the Oneness, the eye, and no-self, there seemed to be no true relationship.

Ultimately I discovered that the only resolution to the many questions that arose, is time. Time means change, and in the process of change my initial questions either changed, dissolved, or were resolved in the process. I had already learned that thinking never brought about change; consequently, thinking netted me nothing when it came to resolving these questions. Though questions inevitably arose, I soon learned it was important not to give them a premature answer.

In similar fashion, I learned this was also true of my experiences. I discovered that as soon as I invested any value, meaning, or purpose in them, I was losing the pearl of great price by giving them a premature closure. It was only by investing no value in an experience that I was able to find out its truth or falsity. What is false never lasts, it falls away of its own accord; while what is true, remains, because truth does not come and go—it is always there. So as long as our experiences come and go and we are investing in them our own values, thoughts, and emotions, we'll never find out if there is any truth in them, for truth is what remains when there are no experiences left.

I only mention this because it was one of the lessons I learned in the mountains. I learned that without any movement, reaction, or response from within (or from self) all experiences were becoming like water on a duck's back. It was as if I had become an outside observer on the relative aspects of life, aspects in which I participated through conditioned habit, while at the same time, participating in the inexplicable reality of the flow of life—true life. It seems that beyond self the relativity of our experiences fall away because there is nothing within that can respond, nothing to hold onto an experience in order to give it value, meaning, and so on. In this way, experiences lose their relative aspects when there is nothing to which they can be relative. This is why, when there is no self, there also seem to be no experiences—no movement, feelings, excitement, or the thousand responses of which the self is capable. From here on, all experiences are of a non-relative character—meaning, the experience is *it*, and there is nothing outside itself.

Since this is difficult to explain, I will give an example of how I came by this understanding. In the following experience I realized the great importance of having no self and of giving no heed to even the most marvelous of events.

The northeast portion of my camp sloped to a small meadow. Directly across, the meadow gave way to a steep descent that led to a lower valley. From the top of the descent a stream gushed from the side of the mountain having made its way underground from a lake a half mile away. Near the outlet of the stream, one could get a view of the valley and surrounding hills laden with boulders, trees, and patches of wild grass. The east wall of this valley was a tall imposing mountain of solid rock that turned red in the sunset. The locals called it "Thunder Mountain."

I often went to this spot, not only to take in the view but to watch for the animals that came to drink. This day, however, I had been collecting firewood and only stopped to rest. Since there was nothing unusual going on at the stream, I stood looking out over the valley, gazing at nothing in particular, when I noticed a peculiar gathering of intensity in the air somewhere over the valley. Whatever it was, it was gathering itself together from all parts and in doing so, was expanding outwards, obliterating everything in its path. At the same time, it grew to such a pitch of vibratory, almost electrical, intensity that it exerted a magnetic pull on my body. At first glimpse it appeared to be the familiar Oneness, but as it grew in intensity I realized it was something else, something I did not recognize at all. The Oneness had always revealed itself through the medium of form, but if this was the Oneness, it now had no medium and was magnified a thousand times over, a magnification that could not be endured. But whatever its reality, I knew that to be caught in the path of its expansion was to be drawn into it like a speck of dust. I thought my time had come and that despite the mystery of what remained, it would remain no longer. Another second and the light would go out forever—the light of the eye that beheld this wonder. Somehow I knew this should not be, yet there was nothing that could be done. I could not look away for there was nowhere else to look, there was no energy to move, within, all was still and motionless—no response, no thoughts, no feelings. What would be, would be.

At the threshold of disintegration something happened. With nothing more to guide it than itself, the body turned away, made an about-face that once more confronted it with the forest and the wood to be gathered. So I went on my way, but did not get far before I had to sit down. The body was so weak and shaken I thought it might yet fall apart, disintegrate.

This experience occurred a number of times while I was in the mountains and each time I could not get over the mechanism of "turning away." Though I was being pulled in the direction of this intensity, of myself I could not have pulled away or turned away. Yet of its own accord, the body turned, and always at the last moment. That the body had a power and wisdom of its own, struck me as a great mystery, a miracle in experience.

I never knew how to evaluate this experience, but each time it occurred I thought the end had come and that the light would go out forever. This would have meant a total blackout such as I had experienced before, a blackout in which there is absolutely nothing, an annihilation more complete than just the loss of self—and what this meant, I had no idea.

I felt the need of great strength to enter the intensity without the light going out, but what kind of strength is this and how could it be acquired? Perhaps it was the strength needed to bear the vision—to enter into God—but I did not know for sure, nor could I imagine how one could see God face to face and live. To come upon such a requirement could make a man despair and turn away. Nevertheless, I felt sure that whatever had brought me this far would give me the strength to go all the way. In my journal I called this experience a "crack in the door."

Chapter 4

The snows came early that year. After two stormy days, I awoke in the night to hear a great silence—a silence only snow can bring. The storm left a foot of snow that so transformed the woods and surrounding mountains it was like a totally new terrain, a place I had never been before. For several days the roads were snowbound, but by the time the snow had partially melted, black heavy clouds hung low above the trees, and when the Ranger's car drove up, I knew what he was going to say.

From time to time the Ranger stopped by to swap animal stories, and each time he never failed to tell a story of someone he'd had to "dig out" because he stayed too long. Since another snowfall was imminent, it was necessary to leave before the roads iced up and I would be snowbound, for how long this time, he did not know.

So after packing my gear and stuffing the remaining nuts into the hollows and holes of my forest friends, I stood there taking a last look around, knowing the best months of my life had come to an end, an end that had been inevitable from the beginning. I knew that although I should return many times to this spot, it would never be the same. I had learned long ago that the es-

sence of life's movement was not contentment or security; rather, it was growth, change, and challenge,
wherein the external circumstances of life merely reflected the needs of each moment in the thrust of life's
flow. What I would find down the mountain I did not
know, but I was sure nothing could ever again alter the
flow I had discovered in the mountains, a flow that
would continue to take me "whithersoever it goeth."

My first destination was a campground overlooking the sea. As beautiful a site as it was, I seemed unable
to appreciate the surroundings because I noticed a subtle change in the object now being picked up by the 3D
glasses. Instead of seeing the Oneness into which all
separateness dissolved, everything now dissolved into
an inexplicable emptiness. Where, for so many months
there had been "something," now there was nothing. In
time, this emptiness became increasingly pronounced
and difficult to live with. Without an "inner" life or the
slightest movement within, "seeing" had become my
life; I was totally dependent upon it, and without it, I
had not a thing to fall back on.

But if the constant sight of emptiness was tedious
and difficult to live with, it was as nothing compared to
what I came upon one morning as I walked along the
beach. Suddenly I was aware that all life around me had
come to a complete standstill. Everywhere I looked, instead of life, I saw a hideous nothingness invading and
strangling the life out of every object and vista in sight.
It was a world being choked to death by an insidious
void whereby every remaining movement was but the
final throe of death. The sudden withdrawal of life, left
in its wake a scene of death, dying and decay so mon-

strous and terrible to look upon, I thought to myself: no man can see this and live! My body froze to the spot.

The immediate reaction was to ward off the view, to make the vision go away by finding some explanation or meaning for it; in a word, to rationalize it away. But as I reached for each defense, the knowledge that I had not a single weapon dawned on me like a sudden blow to the head, and in the same instant I understood this thing called self: it is man's defense against seeing absolute nothingness, against seeing a world devoid of life—a life devoid of God. Without a self, man is defenseless against such a vision, a vision he cannot possibly live with.

Realizing I could no longer project a single defense, I waited for some reaction, especially an inner movement of fear. Somehow I knew that with the birth of fear, self would spring alive with all its weaponry, for it was now obvious that fear—the mother of all inventions—was the core around which the self was built and upon which its life so depended, that self and fear were here, all but indistinguishable. But when no reaction came, when there was no movement of fear, I concluded that self had been frozen and entombed within me in full consciousness of its state of immobility, death, and total helplessness. Unwittingly I had been lured and entrapped in this monstrous state of no-self, an irreversible state because, once gone, the self can never return. Thus in these moments, surrounded by a terror I could not feel, and from which I could not escape, I seemed doomed to remain in the unlivable condition of having to stare out at a horrible nothingness without a single weapon of defense.

Until this moment I had given no thought to the self, or where it had gone the year before; rather, my concern was what remained in its absence. From the time of its disappearance I had known a great freedom—the freedom to come upon the Oneness which lies beyond self. But right now, the silence within was not seen as freedom from self, rather, it was seen as an imprisoned self, a frozen, immovable self that was all part of the scene, part of the insidious nothingness choking the life out of everything. Even now it had frozen my body to the spot. How could I survive another moment?

It seems the one remaining resource was my two legs, two legs that could still run even though they felt frozen and immobile. I had learned before how to move without any need for personal volition—which is to act instantly, without thinking, without any need for self-consciousness or will-power. Once again it worked, and I found myself running down the beach, but as I did so, it was as if something else was running with me, urging, forcing me beyond all physical endurance to "Run! Run as you've never run before! You are running for your life!" And I believed it.

Now I wasn't even a jogger, and there was two miles to go, some of it up a steep cliff; but when I reached my car I seemed mindless of any exhaustion. Jumping in, I drove downtown and parked near the main intersection. I had decided to spend the rest of the day walking and being among my own kind—and it was good to be there.

Since this was a university town, the downtown section was full of young people. On the sidewalk of one corner a jazz-band was playing with full amplifiers;

further on was a more subdued trio; and further yet, a solitary fiddler was playing lively Irish tunes. The shop windows were dressed with outlandish, unique Halloween costumes, and the cafes were crowded. The bookstores, however, were as quiet as a library and in these places I didn't spend much time, but squeezed myself into one of the noisy cafes and ordered a beer. While sitting there watching the people around me, I decided that having no-self was as bad, if not worse, than having a self; because once beyond the self, man was just as likely to come across an unlivable nothingness as he was a marvelous, unnameable "something"—as I first seemed to do. To put aside the self is a premature laying down of our weapons before we know for sure what lies ahead. It's all an insane risk. Without a self, man is totally vulnerable to the winds of chance—bode they good or ill. Looking at the young people around me, I was glad they had a self; in fact, the greatest blessing I could wish upon all the peoples of the earth was to have a self. That way, they would never be able to see what I had just seen and what no man could see and live with.

For myself, of course, it was too late. I had survived this time, but who knows what tomorrow may bring? Fortunately I could not think a moment ahead or imagine how anything more could go wrong; instead, I tried to figure out where, in the past, I had somehow made a wrong turn that had brought me to such an impasse and landed me in this terrible predicament. All I could think of was that I had trusted God too much ...but is that really possible?

I used to wonder if we could ever abandon too much of our self to God, or if there was a limit beyond which a man should not go. Should we abandon our mind, our memory, our whole existence—forfeit all we know in order to come upon Him, the Unknown? It is one thing to abandon our will in the form of accepting trials and tribulations, but it is quite another to be without a will or any energy to call our own. To give one's self to God is one thing, but to have him accept it, is a terrible thing—or so I now understood. The whole problem is that I had given myself to "something" I didn't really know, and why I did not anticipate the present outcome is something else I didn't know. Thus, there was only one way to account for this predicament: in thinking I had abandoned myself to God, I had, in reality, abandoned myself to nothing. So, yes indeed, it is possible to trust God too much, but only if there is no God, only if there is nothing beyond the self.

But if there is no God, then all along I had only been trusting myself—so which was worse? Somehow they both had a way of leading to similar dead ends. But if you can't trust either of these, what's left? That was the real question: if there is no self and no God, what then? I had just seen "what then" and couldn't live with that either. There's nothing blissful about sheer nothingness—even Sartre declared it nauseous—so what it all boils down to is the fact that the only thing we can trust in life is ... well, money.

With a self or without a self, with a belief or without a belief, to survive, man needs money or material goods; it's the ultimate compensation, perhaps, for having no self and no God. We blame greed on the self, but it may not work that way at all; materialism may not stem from the self but from the nothingness that lies beyond the self. So when there is no self and no God what else can we do with our lives but make them economically feasible? And for myself, I thought the sooner I got into this financial game the better off I'd be—after all, life must go on despite our worst experiences of it.

Back at camp, however, I was not so optimistic. I had a messed-up life on my hands and coping with the here-and-now made for some very bad days. I tried to keep busy so as not to remember what had happened and, above all, I stayed away from the beaches because there was no life there anymore. What I had to deal with now, was this frozen self, the very idea of which could be personified as "icy fingers" of an unknown terror and dread that had a way of appearing when my mind was unoccupied. Though seemingly held in abeyance and never approaching too close, I knew they were lurking in the background of my mind and were liable to appear at any time. Right here, I realized how totally my life depended upon the toughness of the immovable stillness within; I knew that the slightest feeling of fear or panic and these icy fingers—which were like sudden flashes of light in my head—would invade my entire being, resulting in madness. But I had no control over this silence, it wasn't even me, rather, it was all that remained of a self-that-was. Thus my fate now lay in the precarious balance between the stillness within and an unknowable terror that could suddenly appear in my mind.

To avoid any possible confrontation I tried, as I have said, to keep very busy, and with four children this was not hard to do. More than once they had been my lifesavers, for despite all the quarreling, dirty rooms, and loud music, they always kept my feet on the ground and my nose to the grindstone. Right now, just being around them was all that mattered. Consequently, an upcoming date to make a retreat with the Hermit Monks on the Big Sur had to be canceled; the last thing I needed was solitude and silence. So I got on the phone and told Brother there was no possible way my present car could make it up their steep hill. He laughed and said, "If you could see some of the 'things' that make it up this hill you'd have to believe in miracles; besides, if you can't make it up, leave the car down and we'll send Brother E to pick you up." So that was that. How could I possibly tell him about these "icy fingers" following me around? For sure he would have told me to go to the hospital instead.

The day I drove down the coast, a big storm hit the Big Sur. Twice I had to pull over and wait for a lull in order to see beyond the windshield. After the second pull-over, I decided to stop at the next phone and tell them I couldn't make it; if it was this bad down the hill, imagine what it must be like going up the hill! Unfortunately, the storm suddenly abated, and by the time I arrived at the foot of the monks' grade it had become a clear and beautiful day.

I decided to wait for Brother E who came down every day at noon to meet the mailman; I thought he could follow me up and be of help should I have any trouble. After helping him unload the pig slop—which the monks donate to their neighboring farmer—Brother got in his car and told me to follow, "In case," he said, "you have any trouble, at least I can keep going!"

At first everything went okay, but when we got to the worst vertical upgrade, Brother suddenly set his brakes, got out of the car, came back and told me to do the same, because he had to put a new blade on his tractor—which was to the right of us, half over the cliff already. Now I did not know if my hand-brake would hold, in fact I was not sure how long the foot-brake would hold, so I shouted at him to "Move it over because I'm going through!" But how could he move over? To the immediate left was a steep embankment, and to the right, a sheer drop; it was obvious that somebody had to give. What happened next could be called the "big squeeze," but once beyond this delay, the rest of the way up was a breeze.

Arriving on top, instead of being relieved, however, I saw the whole situation as positively ludicrous; after all, my car was probably in better shape than some of the clunkers the monks were driving. Then too, since my last trip, the road had been newly paved. So there I stood, possibly the most reluctant retreatant ever to come up the hill, and had I known what lay ahead I would have gone back down. We never know the time or place where our destiny will catch up with us, nor could I have imagined why, for me, it would be here on the monks' hillside.

The first two or three days went by so well, I thought I had finally won out; but on the afternoon of the third or fourth day the icy fingers came back, and in a moment of bravado I decided it was time to have it out with whatever it was. I could not keep running from this thing all my life, I had to get it out in the open, face it head-on and deal with it, because I could no longer stand its continual lurking around every corner of my day. I decided to go outside, sit on the hillside, and stare it in the face until one of us gave way—or went away.

Now I cannot convey what it is like to stare at some invisible horror when you don't know what it is.

Just knowing what it is may be all the defense you need; but when you've gone through your list of name-calling and it does no good, you just have to resign yourself to not knowing and face it anyway. This thing I had to stare down was simply a composite of every connotation we have of "terror," "dread," "fear," "insanity," and things of this order. In a word, it was a mental, psychological killer. Although I knew this whole drama was only in my head, my thinking mind was all but numb in its presence; but for this reason, the thing seemed wholly on the outside so I could personify it as icy fingers, which were like darting tentacles of light. Though it was unlocalized, it was easy to stare at because it was all around me, there was no place else to look.

At one point I thought it might be a raving, maniacal self wanting to get back in. At other times it seemed only to be the fear of having a stroke or fear of insanity; again, it might only be the menopause. But I'm convinced it wouldn't have done the least good to know; by this time absolutely nothing could be done about it, whatever its mission in my life, it was going to be accomplished right here and now.

The longer I watched these fingers the closer they approached, sometimes almost touching, then suddenly retracting; they seemed to be in constant movement (in my mind). Initially, my reaction was only the appearance of goose bumps with a shudder now and then, but later my head grew hot, so hot, in fact, it felt like it was on fire and visually, all I could see were stars. Then I felt my feet begin to freeze with the freezing sensation spreading upward to encompass all but my head. Finally I fell back against the hill in a convulsive condition with my heart beating wildly.

I knew I was going to crack, crack wide open, but never having done this before I had no idea what would happen. I lay there waiting, endlessly waiting for the crack to occur while, physically, this thing was tearing me to pieces. Within, there was not a single movement, not a fear, not a feeling of any kind. At times I tried to focus on this great stillness, but it never gave me any sense of strength or confidence; instead, it was as unconcerned as if a mere fly were buzzing overhead. It seems that the body had been left to bear the brunt of an assault which neither the mind nor the emotions could take part in. Yet, had they been there, the result might have been worse—I do not know. But so bad was my physical condition, I never doubted for a moment that only a miracle could save me; yet, I never expected one, didn't even hope for one, nor could my mind have formulated the simplest prayer. All I wanted to do was get it over with—to die if necessary.

I was not aware of the moment when the dreadful thing departed, for the next thing I was aware of was a profound stillness wherein there was no physical sensation at all. After a while, something must have turned my head because I found myself looking eye-level at a small, yellow wild flower no more than twelve inches away. I cannot describe that moment of seeing, words could never do it justice. Let us just say it smiled—like a smile of welcome from the whole universe. In the intensity of the smile the light of the eye did not go out, nor was there a physical body to turn away; finally, the great intensity could be endured.

It took a while to realize my body was still lying on the hill because, initially, I seemed not to have one. For all I knew I could have been a weed or a pebble on the hillside. After a time, however, the body became obvious and I decided to test it, to see if it was intended to move again. Once more it moved without thought, only this time, the return of physical sensation was accompanied by a mild shock. When I got to my feet it was gratifying to feel the body as relaxed as if nothing had happened. Thus I climbed the hill the same as I had gone down the hill, but only physically, for in reality, something had gone down the hill that never returned.

Apart from the absence of the dreadful thing which I never saw again, I came up the hill without any sense of true existence. Though I searched everywhere in what should have been my being, I now felt there was nothing substantial there, nothing left that I had not experienced as either dissolving or suddenly disappearing, leaving nothing in its place. As for "that" which remained, I had no idea what it was, or even, if it was. Though something obviously climbed the hill, it would be a long time before I discovered its true nature; for the moment, all I knew was that a great change had taken place. In retrospect, I came to regard this event on the hillside as an initiation into what I have called "The Great Passageway," an unusual state of existence—to be described in the next chapter.

A few days after this event, I found myself complaining to Father L that I couldn't keep hold on my existence anymore. So he asked me, "Well, what about your empirical existence—your empirical self—is it sitting here talking to me or not?" I told him, "Visually it would appear to be so, but if I close my eyes, I can't see it anymore." Then I told him of how, during prayer or any time I was inactive, my body would melt away, or seem to dissolve so that if I did not keep my eyes on it, I wouldn't know I had one. With that he threw up his arms and said, "Oh, God, that's far out!" But while I went on complaining, he sat there musing to himself about what would happen to scholastic theology if science proved there was no such thing as a permanent substance in matter.

Eventually I found myself trying to reassure him. I suggested that man's notion of matter-versus-spirit might turn out to be the reverse of what it has traditionally been thought to be; namely, God might turn out to be pure matter or permanent substance, and matter might turn out to be pure spirit or God; in other words, matter and spirit may actually be identical. What this would mean is that the scientist turns out to be the contemplative, or deep-sea fish swimming around looking for the Sea he is already in; while the contemplative turns out to be the unwitting scientist who has already come upon pure substance without realizing it.

But Father wasn't listening;, he was off on one of his theological head-trips, and I knew where it would end. He would eventually draw a blank and then just sit there and stare out the window, over the hillside, and out to the sea into which every theory and insight has a way of eventually dissolving and disappearing. So I left him to discover his own dead ends and went on my way to figure out: how one's body could be visibly apparent as long as the eyes were open, but in no way apparent when the eyes were closed.

Perhaps I should add that the continual melting away of the body was very different from an out-of-the-body experience. While these latter experiences seemingly reveal a division between body and spirit, in my experience there was no such division. Self is responsible for all divisions, but when there was no self there is nothing left to be divided or nothing left to cause division. Because of these experiences, however, I eventually came to look upon the body—as well as all visible form—as somewhat ethereal in nature. Because form itself is composed of an unknowable, untouchable substance that remains permanent throughout all change, it seemed to me it was this substance that remained in the absence of self. At any rate, the whole empirical argument for self-existence melted away once and for all on the hillside, and to this day remains irretrievable.

Before venturing further, I must mention that there was a certain irony in the above event taking place on the monks' hillside. Some two years before, when the monks first opened their retreat house to women, it was first necessary to gain permission from the prior of the monastery—to be screened, in other words. To do this, I made a special trip down the coast for my first meeting with Father Prior who, after graciously giving his permission, asked me, "Well, what do you hope to gain by making a retreat with us?" I told him I didn't know for sure, but for the last year I had felt, interiorly, as if I were getting ready for a great explosion ... when suddenly he stiffened in his chair. "Oh, for God's sake don't do it here!" he said, "We're just trying to get the monks used to having women around and that would ruin it, literally 'blow it' for everyone."

Now I had no idea what Father Prior thought I meant by a "great explosion," but knowing he had been a doctor of chemistry before becoming a monk, I thought he must have had some bad experiences that might have colored any other connotation of the term. For me, the great explosion was supposed to have been a marvelous spiritual blossoming—preferably one with creative overtones. Never in my wildest dreams did I suspect it was my 'self' about to be blasted into a million irretrievable pieces. Such an expectation was not on my Christian agenda, and to do it on the monks' hillside? Certainly it would have been a disgrace to the whole Church. But as I have said, we never know the time or place when destiny will catch up with us. That I should meet mine on the monks' mountain was certainly an ironical event, one I could not have foreseen, but one that was not lost on me.

Chapter 5

Although the mechanisms of change that occurred during the journey are unknown to me, I was immediately able to recognize either the presence of something new or the absence of something old; and the change that took place on the hillside—which began the second half of this journey—can best be understood in relation to the changes that occurred at the beginning.

Initially, with the falling away of all sense of having an interior life, there had been a turning outward to the seeing of Oneness and the falling away of everything particular and individual. The seeing itself was not located within, but first seemed to be like 3D glasses imposed upon my ordinary vision, and later, localized as a seeing "on top of the head." Acclimating to this new outward way of life lasted almost a year before a second major change occurred on the monks' hillside. The essence of this second change was a doing away with everything on the outside, which meant a disappearance of the great Oneness I had seen, as well as the 3D glasses that could now no longer focus on a single object. Thus the seeing, no longer localized, was like a faculty suddenly struck blind. Altogether this adds up to living in a state wherein there is nothing on the inside and nothing on the outside; it's a state of total unknowing and a very difficult state to live in and cope with; however, I shall try to describe it.

Initially, the experience of finding emptiness everywhere I looked had been merely bewildering because it was relatively new. No doubt, the reason my mind could no longer focus on particular objects was due to the total emptiness I found there—an emptiness that no longer gave way or dissolved into Oneness. But as the days and weeks went by without any let-up or compensation, this state of affairs became increasingly difficult to live with. The continual seeing of sheer nothingness within and without makes for an unspeakable sterility, an unendurable mode of existence.

After a time I felt as if my head (my mind, my brain) had been placed in a vise so I could no longer move it at all. I could not look backward to the past, or from side to side in my desperate attempts to focus on something in the immediate present. All I could do was look straight ahead; but straight ahead there was nothing to see, for I felt I had been blindfolded so that before me was only a dark, empty void.

Because my mind could focus on nothing—or hang on to anything knowable—it soon felt as if my brain was on fire or that some terrible pressure behind the eyes was forcing me to go blind. This relentless pressure in my head was like a terrible taskmaster constantly commanding me to "See! You MUST see! You CAN see!" It pounded away day after day, week after week, month after month, until I knew I would never be released from this horrible condition or escape the terrible taskmaster unless I did, eventually, "see." But see what? What was I supposed to be looking for? And how could I ever see when I no longer had eyes to see? Constantly before me there was only emptiness and nothingness.

Because of its terrible restrictiveness I called this state of affairs "The Great Passageway." I had no idea where I was or where I was going. If the first part of the journey was, in fact, the movement from self to no-self, this second half was the movement from no-self to nowhere, for I do not believe self enters the Passageway because it could not endure what must here be endured.

Instinctively I knew this was a very dangerous condition. I felt I was treading on the brink of insanity or some narrow precipice between life and death, and that survival was totally dependent upon no-self—that tough, immovable stillness of everything within. Somehow I knew that the slightest movement within might suddenly throw me off balance and I would slip away forever.

At times it was tempting to regard this great stillness as God, but I think I was mistaken and later shall explain why. Another temptation was to regard the terrible taskmaster as possibly God, for despite its relentless, merciless, non-compensatory commands to "see" and "KEEP GOING," I instinctively felt it knew where it was going and what it was doing. There were moments when I thought of going in search of some type of medication to relieve my burning brain, but since I had never taken drugs in my life, I had no idea what they might do; furthermore, I knew that drugs themselves know not what they do, nor could I believe any doctor knew any more than his drugs. So I trusted the taskmaster to bring me through in order for the journey to take its own course and end in its own time; otherwise, to abort it for any reason might mean never completing the Passage and never knowing what, if anything, lay on the other side.

Another reason I discounted the use of drugs was that I felt the greatest need to stay constantly awake and alert at a time when my personal energies were at the lowest possible ebb. On one such occasion I merely watched—as an unmoved observer watches a light grow distant and fade away altogether—the choiceless ebbing away of the last ounce of physical energy I had. It was then I learned that the passing away and becoming of anything is not the way life really works; for despite the coming and going of what we call life and energy, something remains that never moves nor participates in these passages. Something that is just there, just watching, and "that" is true life, while all the energies that come and go are not true life. But what is "that" that remains and observes? And what is it that endures this passage? What is this form that keeps melting away? And what is it that remains when there is no self? Certainly it was not me. Could it be God then? Well, if it was, I did not know for I could not see a single thing.

This observing of my own coming and going taught me an important lesson. It taught me the meaning of the taskmaster's urgent insistence to "Keep going! Move straight ahead! Don't stop for anything!" which I never understood until this occasion. In watching the final ebbing away of life, I felt absolutely no concern. Nothing in me responded to this observation until it finally occurred to me that at some point I might be going, and never again be coming. But such a prospect can hardly be frightening to a dead man; I had not sufficient energy to care. My life was now in the hands of some mysterious fate and there was no choice but to let the chips fall where they may. But even in such a choiceless moment as death, I knew I had not yet seen, and that there was no way I would be allowed to slip away forever until the journey had been completed. Thus, I realized I would somehow have to keep going, keep dragging my feet, for even if I couldn't see how this passage could possibly be completed in the here-and-now, the prospect of spending a sightless eternity was equally unappealing. But how to keep going was one of the most difficult and trying aspects of the Passageway; yet it was a time of learning how to survive without having the slightest sense of personal energy.

To begin with, I found it necessary to keep constantly occupied with resources outside my own mind, for in this Passageway I could not truly think, reflect, or formulate a single idea or thought. Yet I suddenly discovered I could listen to the thoughts and ideas of others while maintaining a perfectly silent and unthinking mind, for my understanding of practical affairs was unimpaired. As long as I listened, my mind was silent and there was no pressure on it to "be silent." From here, I next discovered I could also read books that demanded no thinking and that left my mind without pressure. Though I couldn't handle philosophy, I found it helpful as well as interesting to read every book on mountain climbing the library had to offer.

Finally, the day came when I discovered I could also talk and converse with this same silent, unthinking mind, but only as long as it came right "off the top"— that is, spontaneously, without thinking or reflecting. At first, such conversations were necessarily brief and limited to practical affairs, but in time, the knack of talking off the top of the head became a permanent function. Later I called it my "non-reflective mind" and gradually recognized it as far superior to the ordinary thinking mind because it allows a great clarity—which I shall try to describe further on.

Right now, however, I was just beginning to discover listening and reading as a way to ward off the pressure in my brain. In a word, I was slowly learning how to cope with life in the Passageway so as to keep going and thus avoid the danger of inactivity, passivity, and non-doing.

It was due to these dangers that I eventually came upon a new type of activity, the activity of an unthinking, unknowing mind in which there are no self-invested energies, no goal but survival, and not an ounce of satisfaction anywhere. It was right here—unknown to me at the time—that I was beginning to emerge into a whole new way of life which no intellect can fashion or even imagine possible until it comes upon this life from the other side of knowing—which is from the side of unknowing.

The worst part of the Passageway, by far, was its non-compensatory aspect, as well as its four month duration. A few days or weeks, okay, but almost four full months of being in a mental straitjacket verged day after day on the brink of the intolerable. Years before I had come upon a passage in a book describing a state of unknowing which the author defined as "complete psychological dissociation without compensation" or some such phrase as that. At the time I could not imagine what he was talking about, but felt sure it was something terrible and was glad I had never known any condition as dire as this sounded. But here, during the Passage, I recalled the statement because it seemed to epitomize my present situation better than any words my mind could formulate. Though I do not know its psychological usage—the author was a psychologist—I took it for my own condition of being completely cut off (dissociated) from the known, the self, without any compensating factor to take the place of the void so encountered. It meant a state of no feelings, no energies, no movements, no insights, no seeing, no relationships with anything, nothing but absolute emptiness everywhere you turn. The utter sterility of this state is all but humanly unendurable, especially for any length of time; to bear the burden of complete unknowing is a weight that moment by moment threatened to crush me, but crush me without bringing death. I had already seen that death was no release because sooner or later the Passageway must be completed, and I would never be free of the burden of unknowing until I could see.

This state cannot be compared to a Dark Night, it is more (and far worse) than the purification of the mind and will in its ignorance of the Unknown; rather, it is a radical state wherein the mind cannot dwell on anything known or unknown. Although empirical reality remained, it could not be focused on perceptually, nor could individual objects even be focused on visually. Instead, the usual objects of mind and sense were seen in a global sense, which made for some tense moments, particularly when driving or shopping in a market. Such a state might be akin to the infant's outlook on the world wherein he visually sees what the adult sees, but lacks the adult's perception and focusing ability because his mind is still in the non-relative state of unknowing.

But for the adult, relative, knowing mind, to return to this non-relative condition while maintaining itself within the range of normalcy, is a feat of gigantic proportions. Yet, oddly enough, the saving grace—at least grace that is knowable and obvious—is the conditioned mind itself.

I had always been antipathetic toward the behaviorists' conditioned model of human thought and behavior, but in the Passageway I understood its importance as the very condition of sanity, and that the preconditioned habits of a balanced, integrated, adult mind were absolutely essential for making the passage. Hence, the years prior to taking the journey—years of trying and testing the psychic balance—were of the utmost importance; so much so that everything now depended upon this stability of conditioned behavior. With only two or three exceptions, I experienced nothing that could be called a divine, strengthening grace. For the most part, I walked under the weighty, enormous burden of such total unknowing that just the ability to keep going was beyond comprehension itself.

On the few occasions I came upon divine relief, there was no mistaking its origin. These events occurred toward the end of the Passageway—a fact I can only see in retrospect—and were always preceded by a piling up of all the intolerable aspects of this state: its duration, its apparent endlessness, the fatigue, the pressure behind the eyes, the precarious state of sanity, the total lack of understanding; in a word, the terrible burden of unknowing and unseeing. All this and more, suddenly became overwhelming, and under its monstrous weight, something collapsed. Whatever remains without a self, disintegrated, melted away like the thin-

nest veil to the infinite. It was the obliteration of all but
the joyous, humorous smile of the divine, a smile that
somehow was completely subjective. Its most poignant,
immediate word of description was "melting"—a veritable melting in which God was all that remained.

Despite this momentary reprieve I would soon return to the usual condition and therefore had to discount this as the final seeing. The melting away of what
remained was evidently not the seeing that had been demanded. If anything, it struck me as a merciful scolding
from the taskmaster, as if my own hardness had melted
and it was saying, "I told you, you could see! You are
seeing all the time—and you know this! You cannot
possibly doubt it." Indeed, there was no doubt, the nature of the passage does not permit of intellectual doubt;
but then, neither does it permit of certitude. In truth, it
permits of nothing.

Apart from these too few reprieves, the mind was
immersed in a dire void wherein it had nowhere to look
since it could focus on nothing. Here I was reminded of
Christ's saying he had nowhere to lay his head—meaning there was nothing in this world on which he could
truly focus his attention, nothing to which his mind
could be either perceptually or conceptually attached.

Eventually it became clear that this Passageway
was beyond despair, and even beyond insanity; for
"who" is left to go insane or "what" remains to experience despair? If self had been alive it would have gone
mad on the spot; and if nothing else, it would have
jumped at any chance to throw in the towel and back
out. But our psychological notions of despair and anxiety are mere toys of self-defense compared to the bur-
den-of-unknowing, against which there isn't a single

defense; nor is there, for that matter, anything or anyone left to defend. To have had a self would have been most compensating, for self *is* man's compensation for a state of unknowing—or so I was now convinced.

Nevertheless, the true mechanism of surviving the Passageway is not known to me. Self was dead, immovably silent. The taskmaster (merely a pressure on my brain) kept demanding that my mind be still and "See!" And my body was ingesting health foods in its feeble attempt to compensate for the loss of self-energy. Probably the mechanism of getting through is built into the Passageway itself, if for no other reason than that it's the only way to go. There are no options and no outs, no death and no insanity; it's there and you're part of it, and that's what is—just a Passageway.

By the end of four months I had learned, to some extent, how to cope with this state of affairs. By "cope" I do not mean an act of resignation, but merely an acclimation to the inevitable. For all I knew, I might have to live this way the rest of my life, so I did my best to work up some commensurate routine in order to keep going. Most important, perhaps, is the fact that I eventually became acclimated to the void when I discovered that time alone took care of it, for after a while it was hardly noticed anymore.

It seems that when the emptiness of existence is no longer important, "doing" becomes everything. Thus, during the Passageway the emphasis shifted from simple existence—such as I had known it in the mountains—to doing, which now became a way of life. Nevertheless, during this time, while walking through the hills, I sometimes came upon a certain sadness concerning the rock-bottom emptiness of man and nature. I felt bad about the fact that man lives his whole life in the false expectation that some ultimate reality lies hidden somewhere behind, beneath, or beyond what is. And I remembered my own life of searching and looking and now saw what a complete waste it had been.

All the experiences of my life had been nothing more than a head-trip, a great psychological hoax, a pointless circular affair whereby I was now back where I started—not knowing any more about life or God than the day I was born. To think of all the wasted energy: studying, speculating, practicing, looking, striving, suffering, experiencing, and all of it? A perfect waste! In truth, everything man knows is one hundred percent speculation and wishful thinking, egged blindly on, no doubt, by a self persistently demanding its own survival. What a trick of the mind! What total deception! And what man born has not been led by the nose and fallen into this trap—a trap which *is* the self? And yet, what lies beyond the self? If emptiness and nothingness is the whole truth and nothing but the truth, then man is entitled to his self and his deceptions; he must have this compensation for an ultimate reality that turns out to be sheer nothingness.

Again and again in these walks through the hills and along the river I wondered too, if there was any last vestige in me of "trust in God." Initially I had been willing to give up this thing called self because I was somehow assured that God lay beyond it. So I had trusted and I had loved, and until the Great Passageway had not been deceived. But now that trust had finally been broken to pieces for I could find it nowhere. In its place was a gentle disappointment and the final acceptance of what is—which means: what you see is all you get. It also means just the simple doing of whatever lies before you to do at each moment of the day, with no looking around, searching underneath, or probing behind. Just the doing of what is immediately under your nose to do, and not a thing more.

So this was the end of the line. I had finally come upon the great truth: that all was void; that self had merely filled in the void; and that all man's words were empty labels foraged by a mind that doesn't know a thing about its world and cannot tolerate a state of un-knowing. Well, I could live with this. Although coming upon these great truths had almost cost me my life, finally I was discovering how to live with them; after all, this is what the journey was all about: to find the truth and nothing less. I might continue to be sorry for all those still wasting their lives in the unwitting search for emptiness, yet I felt no zeal to inform them of the truth ahead of time, for knowing the truth doesn't necessarily make for a better life, a life that must go on whether there's any truth in it or not. Thus, with this insight I felt sure I had come full circle and could finally put this whole business aside and go out and make some money.

Chapter 6

It was late winter and the muddy waters of the river were jammed with burnt debris from a mountain fire two years before. Every day my son and I would stand on the banks to measure the height of the swelling waters, and then he would use the swift moving logs as targets for his rocks, for he had a strong pitch and a good eye. One day, however, he was late in coming, so I walked down and sat on the river's edge, watching the dead wood in its speedy descent to the sea. With neither reason nor provocation, a smile emerged on my face, and in the split second of recognition I "saw"—finally I saw and knew I had seen. I knew: *the smile itself, that which smiled, and that at which it smiled, were One*—as indistinguishably one as a trinity without division. And what I saw was merely how this was so. There was no insight, no vision, no movement of anything, but a seeing that was as natural and spontaneous as a smile on a face—not another thing more. In my journal I called this "the grin-of-recognition."

Since what I had seen could not be retained, grasped or held onto by the mind, I continued to watch the river as it cleaned out the mountain debris and washed down the banks in its determined flow to meet with the sea. Later I took a walk and saw that although the Great Passageway was now over, everything looked as usual. Nothing had changed and it was good to see this was so. If there was anything marvelous or spectacular about this seeing it was the fact that everything was as usual and that nothing had changed, because it meant that I too was as usual and had arrived at the end of the passage, normal, whole, and sane. I was grateful for this, it was almost too good to be true; and yet, how could it be otherwise when "that" which remains at the end of the passage is Itself normal, whole, and sane?

It may seem strange to have rejoiced more in the ending of the passage than in what had been revealed there. It must be understood, however, that I could not rejoice in what had been revealed because I could not grasp it or hang on to it. It was so utterly simple and so completely obvious it was impossible to understand why I had not seen it before; and yet, there is no way I could come to this seeing of my own accord—it had to be revealed.

What I learned was that the unknown object (of the smile) was identical with the subject, and not only that, but the smile itself was identical with these—a threesome, in other words. And what is the smile? It is "that" which remains when there is no self. *The smile is neither the unknown subject or object, yet it is identical with it*. It is that aspect of the Unknown which is obviously manifest. The implications of this seeing are tremendous, and yet they cannot be grasped by the mind.

The full implication of this seeing, however, was not immediately apparent. Though the pressure behind the eyes never returned, and my mind knew an effortless silence despite the routine of daily affairs, life went on as usual; I was not aware of any real change. Then, about a week or so later while on my way to catch an early morning bus, the usual void was replaced by something else, something that was not localized as a presence, but something more pervasive and intense than even the Oneness I had seen with the 3D glasses. Immediately I took this for an absolute sham, a trap, a trick of the mind; besides, it came too late, I was now beyond all such enticements that had landed me nothing but trouble in the past. So I ignored it, refused to give it space or look at it; and if I'd had a self, I probably would have felt toward it a feeling of disdain. I walked on, looking straight ahead, and went to work.

But "it" also went to work, and so surrounded me I could hardly divert my eyes from it. This went on for several days until I knew that the greater my attempts to ignore it, the greater it increased the pressure to "Look!" So eventually I did look, and the moment I did so, it vanished and was gone. But in the same instant I knew why.

You cannot look at what Is, for it cannot become an object to the mind, nor for that matter, can it be a subject, for what Is is "that" which can never be a subject or an object. Thus the moment you look with your relative (subject-object oriented) mind, what Is is gone because you have tried to make it an object, and it won't work—why? Because there is no subject. The relative mind cannot apprehend this reality; only a non-relative mind sees because what Is is equally non-reflective or non-self-conscious. Since what Is is all that Is, it has nothing to see outside itself nor within itself, and thus it has no such thing as a relative, reflective, self-conscious mind. Nor is it a mind at all, nor consciousness, for no man knows *what* it is, only *that* it Is. Therefore, once we have been rid of a reflective, relative, self-conscious mind, then and only then can we come upon what Is, which is neither subject nor object, but "seeing" Itself. [1]

It seems the pressure to "look" was a pressure on the relative mind that was seemingly put out of commission during the Passageway when it was unable to focus on or retain a single object in mind. Thus, when finally and suddenly confronted with something to look at, there was a mental reluctance to do so. It was as if I had been asked to regress or look backward, and I was extremely wary of doing so; after all, I didn't want to go on any more journeys if I didn't have to. Nevertheless, my eventual looking served a great purpose and brought about the change which the initial seeing by the river could not do.

Once I realized that what Is can never be an object to Itself (and thus, never a subject), I had the marvelous and unique key to seeing it all the time—which was by not looking at all. It was as if the moment of its vanish-

---

[1] Needless to say, all references to "object" in this book refer to the object of consciousness, not to an object of the senses. The immediate object of consciousness is always and only itself; whereas the object of the senses is anything we can see, hear or touch. Failure to distinguish the object of consciousness (self or subject) from sensory objects—trees, mountains, and you name it—has been the cause of some confusion in contemplative literature. Thus when the contemplative refers to God as "object" he is referring to God as the primary object of consciousness, not to God as an object of the senses. Beyond consciousness, however, there is neither subject nor object— no self and no God. Beyond this, Truth is its own revelation and manifestation, there being no one (no consciousness) *to* which it is revealed. The mind, however, cannot comprehend or grasp this non-subjective, non-objective Truth.

ing was also the final and complete close-down of the relative mind, which then heralded a new way of seeing, knowing, and acting because now, I had the key! Now I could understand, and because of this, now I could rejoice. It seems that as long as the mind is viable it needs to enter into some form of understanding, otherwise the greatest revelation, while it would not go unnoticed, could not enter into the fullness of its human manifestation.

Part of what I understood is how what Is never comes and goes; instead, what comes and goes is the relative mind that is intimately entwined with the self, revolves around the self, and of its own accord can never get out of itself. But once the self has disappeared, this reflective, self-conscious mind goes with it, and what remains is what Is. You can no longer look out and see relationships, nor do you see emptiness anymore, all you see is what Is, which can be intense at times, even though it is not something ecstatic, ineffable, or transcendent. On the contrary, it is obvious, natural, and somewhat ordinary, for it is what we see everywhere we look—and yet, how difficult it is to see how this is so! Though what Is is everything that truly exists, there is one thing it is not, and that is self, which blocks the view that otherwise allows us to see that which remains when self is gone—namely, what Is.

This discovery then, was the end of the Passageway, and once I began to see, another new way of life opened up. There were more months of acclimating during which I came upon many discoveries, the nature of which is difficult to communicate, even though I must try. The key discovery is what I call "doing," which seems to take the place of willing or that energy we once experienced as life and being. Doing is an energyless, non-reflective, effortless activity that must be distinguished from a deliberate, self-aware type of activity that needs constant effort and maintenance. For this reason, doing is nothing we can bring about by our own efforts and energies because doing is what follows automatically when all personal efforts and energies have ceased. The term "effortless" here refers to the fact that no self-energies are involved even though, physically, we may still work up a sweat.

Learning to distinguish doing from past methods of activity is much like the conditioning process every child is taught by its parents. In this case, any attempt in self-invested activity results in emptiness because there is nothing there; whereas, with activity in which there is no self-investment or self-awareness, *something* is there; this activity is not empty and is what I call "doing." The reason for using this term is because the doer, as well as that which the doer acts upon, falls into the realm of the unknown; only the act of doing falls into the realm of the known. We do not know "that" which smiled or at "what" it smiled, all we know is the smile itself. This means that what Is can only be known because it is identical with its acts (or doing).

Initially, the process of learning the difference between doing and self-activity may be compared to balancing on a walking beam. Where doing means having your foot squarely on target so there is something underfoot, non-doing or self-invested activity finds no foothold because there is nothing underfoot. At first, making your way along this beam is by trial and error, but eventually, walking the beam becomes second nature; or rather, you discover in time that walking this beam is your real nature and the way you must walk for the rest of your life. In this way, when there is something there (underfoot, so to speak) you know you are on beam and are living and doing as you are supposed to be doing; but when there is only a void underfoot, then you are not on beam and there is no real doing. Doing then, is a manifestation of something or what Is, and non-doing (self-invested activity) is the manifestation of absolutely nothing. Where once on this journey the emphasis had been on a selfless existence, this existence was gradually seen to be empty and void and no longer of any use. But when this selfless existence disappears completely, what remains is doing, which is like a beam, a guide, and is the something that is what Is.

The content of doing, or what we do, is mapped out by the unknowable direction of the beam, which is narrow and straight and does not go in any willy-nilly direction. When on beam we are no longer free to come and go because only self enjoys such freedoms. A choiceless state knows nothing of those usual referents of freedom. Here, there is only freedom from the self which turns out to be no freedom at all. Who is there to be free? Who is there to choose and experience, to set the goals and chart the path? The free one is now gone, and that which remains now walks the beam like an unthinking tree must grow and function in a direction already set by its nature, a nature so intelligent that it is forever completely unknowable to the human mind. Thus knowing what to do or where to put your foot is fairly black and white: what is to be known is simply there, and what is not known is not there. In other words, what to do is built into the beam itself so that doing is identical with its content or what it does. Thus, knowing, seeing, doing, are but a single act without a gap between.

What once created the division between doing and its content was the self with all its choices, values, judgments, ideas, and all the rest, which never gets on the beam and can't find it because it is blocked by all its so-called freedoms. Not knowing what to do, what to think, what to say, how to live is, by contrast, a state of perpetual confusion. But on this beam what Is moves in one sure, irrevocable, and unknowable direction, so that knowing and doing are the same. Nevertheless, this knowing is most unusual because it is not derived from a thinking, speculating, reflecting mind. Rather, whatever is before you is something either known or unknown, and in this way many things are now seen as obvious and clear which before could not have been known or seen at all. How this works is unknown to me, but that it works at all is a source of amazement and all part of the clarity of mind now possible when on the beam—which means being totally at one with what Is.

A second discovery occurring in the last months of the journey was coming upon the silent mind. Though I was acquainted with many types of silence and many times had come upon a silent mind, this final silence was unique and different than anything encountered before. Since I would like to try and describe it later at length—because it is so difficult to convey—I will only say for now, the silent mind is a mind that is void of reflexive activity or consciousness, and though all other functions of the mind seem to remain as usual, there is no experience of a mind at all. The reason self cannot come upon this silence is because this silence is what remains when there is no self, or when all self-awareness comes to an end. This is why I had no knowledge of this type of silence prior to taking the journey, and only recognized it for what it was at the very end. What I also discovered at the end was how doing actually takes the place of willing and thinking, and thus leaves the ordinary mind silent.

Since it is difficult to do justice to the many discoveries made possible by this journey, I will only touch upon those which were most surprising and, initially, a bit disconcerting. One such discovery was the falling away of the aesthetic sense, or that particular sense of order, beauty, and harmony we find in nature or in our environment. As a lover of classical music—who thought music might endure beyond the spheres—I was surprised to find that silence surpassed the greatest works of the masters. Though I have no way to account for it, music became noise, and silence became harmony.

I also noticed that when it became impossible to focus on the singularity or discreteness of objects, all sense of their ordered arrangement disappeared. Instead, the contents of the known, with its apparent laws and rules of order, were now seen as a continuous whole, a spontaneous thrust of life which, like a single sustained note, could easily disintegrate if this tension were released. Nothing then, is predictable. That which is manifest is not subject to any rule or law outside itself—however ingenuous and obvious is its visible design.

Of its own accord this way of seeing resulted in a simplified style of life. When there is no beauty, then no object can be valued more than another, and thus every non-utilitarian possession becomes excess baggage. The barest cell and the simple life in the woods now struck me as the only authentic way of life, and if it hadn't been for the children, I would have thrown everything to the wind and gone off. Such an ascetic ending may seem harsh, but the reason nothing in particular is beautiful is because the beauty of what Is overshadows the particularity of all form. Thus visible form is bypassed or overshadowed by the "thing in Itself." Then too, we no longer need to see or possess beauty when we are truly a part of it, or are already possessed by it.

Another discovery occurred when I realized the necessity of taking on some semblance of self-consciousness. This dawned on me when, after spending a day in public and away from home, I saw I had forgotten to comb my hair in the morning—and it looked like hell (pardon the expression). Thereupon I began a concerted program to try and remember myself—to remember anything in fact. By the end of the Passageway I was certain my memory had been impaired for life. It was not a failure in recall, however, but more like time-lapses, as if whole chunks of time were missing from the ordinary flow of life. It was less a forgetfulness of time, however, than it was a forgetfulness of self. Though I tried to find some compensatory measures to insure myself against these lapses, nothing worked. In the long run, time took care of itself because, after a number of years, the practical memory gradually returned, and I was relieved of the impossible effort of remembering myself.

Apparently, with the falling away of self-consciousness there is also a certain loss of body-awareness. This may account for the continual melting away of physical form I experienced during the latter half of the journey. In time, however, I acclimated to getting around this way, or without a certain awareness of physical form. To some extent this means taking better care of the body than ever before because now, the body tells me nothing. Though physical pain remains, there is no longer the feeling of being tired, rested, satisfied, contented, and so much more; somehow these familiar feelings must have subtle connections with self-consciousness. But because of this, caring for the body becomes little different than caring for a plant: when you know it needs water, food, or sunshine, you give it what it needs. You cannot "feel" for the plant, but if you are observant and know something of its mechanism, there is no problem maintaining a bodily form that is in a constant process of change and subject to the limits of time. Though I regard the body as absolutely real, I find all forms that compose the universe extremely fragile or tenuous at best, because they can so easily dissolve into the one Existent, apart from which, no form has any individual existence of its own.

Earlier I said that I often wondered if the indomitable stillness within might not be God. Somehow I seemed to hold to the notion that someday the silence of no-self would give way and reveal itself as the great Unknown—the Divine, whose inflow I had sorely missed in the absence of self. But since all awareness of interior stillness was eventually lost, I discounted this notion because even the silence of no-self no longer existed. However, once the journey was over, I realized that God does not experience himself as anything comparable to the relative experiences of self or no-self, thus I saw how it could, indeed, have been God all along. It seems I had first to recognize this same stillness and emptiness as pervading everything, not just myself, before I saw its connecting link with all that Is. Thus only when I saw how it could never be localized anywhere in particular or in any subjective form, I finally saw how this great silence was indeed Everything and Everywhere, and is truly what Is.

In many ways this journey is comparable to a tree that has suddenly been felled but is not yet dead because the sap (the self) still runs in its veins and only gradually, slowly, comes to a complete halt. At first the tree merely experiences the ebbing and dwindling of its own life-giving energies, and is continually astonished to realize that while it is being emptied, it somehow continues to remain. In this way it discovers that what it once thought necessary for life—the sap—is actually not necessary at all, for even when the sap is totally gone, it does not die. But the process of dying to its ordinary way of life lends an uneasiness to the journey because the tree never knows when, or if, it is dead, since it never experiences the in-flow of new life as the old life flows out. For me, this was the most bewildering aspect of the journey. I had fully expected that as self disappeared some form of divine life would appear and fill in the void. When this didn't happen, I knew I was lost.

In retrospect I now realize the full meaning of John of the Cross' continual statements to his students: that God can never truly be experienced by the faculties of man. Therefore, what we experience of God is frankly ourselves—because self is our only medium of doing so. The mind, will, emotions and feelings, in a word, all our experiences in the interior life are merely our own reactions to "that" which we cannot otherwise know, see, or experience. How often then, have we mistaken ourselves for God? Or possibly, mistaken God for our-

selves? There's only one way to find out, and that is to
have no self at all. Since self cannot experience God as
he truly Is, then the only way to do so is to be prepared
to relinquish every last thing we know as self—everything we experience, in fact.

This explains why there is no experience of any divine inflow or Godlike substitute for a self-that-was, for
such is not the experience of God himself, who is not
self-conscious and does not experience any divine in-
flow. Perhaps this is why we sometimes refer to God as
the great emptiness and nothingness, though God is not
that, not at all. What we call emptiness and nothingness
is self's relative notion and experience, which moves
from the positive to the negative before both eventually
fall away and all that remains is what Is.

Nevertheless, if there is any aspect of this journey
I would stress or emphasize, it is the necessity of finally
coming to terms with the void and nothingness of existence which, for me, seemed to be the equivalent of living
out my life without God or any such substitute. Only
when this came about, when the acclimation to a life
without an ultimate reality was complete, with no hope
or trust remaining, only when I had finally to accept
what is, did I suddenly realize that what is *Is* Truth itself
and all that Is. I had to discover it was only when every
single, subtle experience and thought, conscious and
unconscious, had come to a complete end, it was possible for Truth to reveal itself without any medium—
without self or consciousness, that is.

Although it was impossible to pinpoint the time or
moment when the journey was over, I tend to gauge the
ending when I could no longer find any relative difference between having a self and having no-self, or the

time at which all awareness of the stillness within became lost to me. Originally the awareness of no-self was
merely the awareness of the absence of self with all its
habitual reactions, feelings, movements, thoughts and
experiences. For this reason the awareness of no-self is
purely relative to what was—to self, that is. But as the
distance between the two increases with the acclimating, accommodating process of settling down to a new
way of life, the old life-with-self grows dim and fades
out altogether, and with it, the relative contrast also disappears. This means there is no more awareness of the
silent, still, immovable no-self that was so necessary for
making the journey—especially in the Great Passageway. Thus, with the fading away of no-self I knew the
journey was over; it was now but a past event, and like
all past events, it grows colorless and lifeless as it recedes from memory and loses its relevance for the here-
and-now.

Compendium of the Journey

I

The moment was unheralded, unrecognized, and unknown; it was the moment I entered a great silence and never returned. Beyond the threshold of the known, the door upon self was closed, but the door upon the Unknown was opened in a fixed gaze that could not look away. Impossible to see or remember self or to be self-conscious, the mind was restricted to the present moment. The more it tried to reflect on itself, the more overpowering the silence.

II

By steadily gazing outward upon the Unknown, the silence abated and the emptiness of self became a joy. But the search for the divine center or still-point—God within—revealed not one emptiness, but two, for when there is no self, there is no Other; without a personal self there seems to be no personal God, for without a subject, there can be no object. The still-point or unitive center had vanished, taking with it every sense of life the self possessed—a self which could no longer be felt to exist. What remained was not known. There was no life, no will, no energy, no feelings, no experiences, no within, no spiritual or psychic life. Yet, life was somewhere, because all else went on as usual.

III

Though it could not be localized or found within any object of sight or mind, somewhere out-of-doors life was flowing peacefully, assuredly. On a bluff above the sea it revealed itself: life is not *in* anything; rather, all things are *in* life. The many are immersed in the One, even that which remains when there is no self is absorbed in the One. No longer a distance between self and other, all is now known in the immediacy of this identity. Particulars dissolve into the One, and individual objects give way to reveal that which is the same throughout all variety and multiplicity. To see this new dimension of life is the gift of amazing glasses through which God is not only seen everywhere, but AS Everywhere. Truly, God is all that exists—all, of course, but the self.

IV

But what sees this Oneness and knows that it sees? The eye that looks is not within, it is not of mind or body, it is not of self. Unknown and outside—at first like glasses, and later, above the head—the eye was known to exist, but it could neither be seen or looked at.

It did not dissolve into Oneness—the seer and seen were not identical. But a greater mystery still: what remained in the absence of self? What is this that walks and talks and is aware of the eye upon Oneness? Among them— no-self, the eye, and Oneness—no identity could be found.

V

At one time, the Oneness grew to an overpowering intensity, as if drawing itself together from all parts, drawing inward and obliterating all that existed, including the eye that saw it and that which remained. At the threshold of extinction, the eye flickered and grew dim; instantly, that which remained turned away. To bear the vision, to enter in, the light of the eye must not go out. Somehow it must become stronger, but what kind of strength is this and how could it be acquired? There was something still to be done—but what? No-self is helpless; it has no strength; it is not the light of the eye nor the eye itself.

VI

Nine months passed before the eye upon Oneness became the eye upon nothingness. Without warning or reason, all particulars dissolved into absolute nothingness. At one point, the mind came upon the hideous void of life, the insidious nothingness of death and decay strangling life from every object of sight. Only self can escape such a vision because only self knows fear, and only fear can generate the weapons of defense. Without a self the only escape is no escape; the void must be faced, come what may. On the hillside, the epitome of all that is dreadful and insane is confronted; but who or what beheld this terror, or could endure it? In the absence of self, all that remained was an immovable stillness, an unbreakable, unfeeling silence. Would it move, crack open, or would it hold? This could not be known, surmised or even hoped for. What would be, would be.

VII

The stillness held fast because nothingness cannot know fear or dread. Yet the wild flower yielded, it gave way, expanded infinitely to reveal a great intensity that could now be seen without the eye growing dim or the light going out. The body dissolves and melts into the stillness of what remains. Afterwards, the eye no longer sees anything at all; instead, it presses downward on the mind like a terrible taskmaster demanding that it "See!" The mind can no longer focus on anything in particular or in general, it can see nothing within or without. It is in a state of complete unknowing, a dire state and a Passageway wherein, for months, the mind is fixed in a rigid now-moment out of which it cannot move and in which, there is nothing to see.

VIII

In this Passageway true life, unlocalized and nowhere, reveals itself as that which remains and knows no death. It is this life that continues despite unseeing and unknowing, an eternal life that, strangely, has no God as object of vision. But how can ordinary life go on without the energies of self and when true life has no such energies? How is it possible to stay in the flesh and in the ordinary mind when no life seems to lie therein? The only answer is time—time to grow accustomed, to acclimate, to learn all over again how to live this new life. To do so, self is nowhere, it cannot help; the mind does not know how; and the body keeps melting away.

IX

When the adjustment is made—but barely—the journey appears to be over. At first, the nothingness of existence becomes endurable; later, it is an ordinary sight; and finally, it is so taken for granted it is never noticed or seen again. When nothing moves in to take its place, nothingness becomes all that is; and this, finally, had to be accepted as the most obvious of ultimate truths. Here it could be clearly seen that all the searching, speculating, and experiencing of a lifetime had been a gigantic waste, a head-trip of such proportions that only an infant mentality can bare such a truth: the end is like the beginning, and everything in between is pure deception. The state of unknowing is permanent; since the mind can hold on to no content, there is nothing more that can be learned. There will be no more journeys; this is the last, the end—an end which is absolute nothingness.

X

As the river flows, from out of the formless void arises the greatest of great realities—a simple smile. *The smile itself, the one that smiled and the one at which it smiled were as identical as the trinity.* The smile is neither subject nor object, but the act and manifestation of the otherwise unknown and unmanifest; it is the form of the formless, the Eternal Form from which all multiple form arises and to which it ultimately returns. The true nature, then, of what remains beyond self is Eternal Form—the act and manifestation of the formless and unmanifest. The relative mind cannot hold on to this truth, it cannot grasp, convey—or even believe—that which has revealed itself. This identity can never be communicated because it is the one existent that can never be either objectified or subjectified.

XI

Later, after its four-month absence, the Oneness reappeared, but no longer through the medium of particular form. But its return was too late; something had now been revealed, compared to which, all else was but a deception. Still, the mind wanted to look, it *had* to

look, and when it did, the Oneness vanished; but instantly, the mind understood why. It understood that
Oneness—what Is or God—can never be the object (or
subject) of vision because it is the Act of vision itself.
Here the gap between the subject and object of the Eye
seeing itself was irrevocably closed; God is neither seer
nor seen, but "seeing." After a long passage, the mind
had finally come to rest and rejoice in its own understanding. Now it was ready and prepared to take its
rightful place in the immediacy and practicality of the
now-moment. There will be no more looking, no need
for the mind to know what it now knows is forever beyond itself. In this unknowing the mind is content to
dwell forever.

XII

Yet another period of acclimating, of adjusting to
the non-relative life beyond the Passageway. Then, just
as self had once faded into silence, so too, the silence and
stillness of no-self faded beyond recognition. The journey—its experiences, insights, and learning devices—
had only been the means of transition from the old to the
new life, from a relative to a non-relative way of knowing and seeing. It was all over now; beyond the relational the Eye seeing itself is never static because its seeing
is so continuously new that the now-moment is never
the same. Since the eternally new is of Its essence, the
journey moves on, eternally onward.

The Silent Mind

I wish I understood the mechanism of self-consciousness or how it is possible for the mind to bend on itself, for if I did, I could more easily convey a better understanding of no-self and its most noticeable effect—the silent mind. But whatever this mechanism is, the state of no-self is the breaking up of a self-conscious system whereafter the mind can no longer see itself as object to itself; and at the same time, it loses the ability to find any other object to take its place, because when there is no self there is also no other.

I might add that the mind has never had the ability to see itself as subject—which would be as impossible as the eye seeing itself. Yet I think this very impossibility may be the clue to the type of knowing that remains when consciousness without a knowable subject or object becomes the whole of it. This type of knowing, however, is not available to our ordinary way of knowing, and because it cannot be experienced or understood by the relative mind, it falls squarely into the realm of the unknown and the unknowable.

I used to believe that in order to know of self's existence, it was not necessary for the mind to reflect on itself or to be an object to itself—be self-conscious, that is.

Instead, I believed that the basic awareness of thoughts
and feelings went right on and were present whether I
reflected on them or not. Now, however, I see how both
of these are true. It seems that on an unconscious level
the reflexive mechanism of the mind goes on so continuously, it makes no difference if we are aware of our self
on a conscious level or not. In other words, the mind is
always bending on itself—and knowing itself as object
to itself—even when we are not aware of it or are unconscious of this fact. This means that if the reflexive mechanism were to be cut off, we would not only lose
awareness of our self on a conscious level, but lose
awareness of self on an unconscious level as well. Stated more simply: *when we can no longer reflect (or check) on
the subject of awareness, we lose consciousness of there being
any subject* —or there being any consciousness at all. To
one who remains self-conscious, of course, this seems
impossible. To such a one, the subject of consciousness
is so evident, experiential and logical, it needs no proof;
in fact, it cannot even be questioned. But to the unself-
conscious mind, no such proof is possible.

The first question to be asked is whether or not
self-consciousness is necessary for thinking, or if thinking goes right on without a thinker. My answer is that
thinking can only arise in a self-conscious mind—which
is why the infant mentality cannot survive in an adult
world. But once the mind is patterned and conditioned,
or brought to its full potential as a functioning mechanism, thinking can go right on without any need for a
self-conscious mechanism. At the same time, however,
it will be a different kind of thinking. Where before,
thought had been a product of a reflecting, introspec-
tive, objectifying mechanism—ever colored with per-

sonal feelings and biases—now whatever is to be known is spontaneously there. Furthermore, the known arises in the now-moment, which is solely concerned with the immediate present, thus making it invariably practical. This is undoubtedly a restrictive state of mind, but it is a blessed restrictiveness. Since the continual movement inward and outward, backward and forward, in time and in the service of feelings, personal projections and so on, is an exhausting state, it consumes an untold amount of energy that is otherwise left free when the mind is restricted to the now-moment.

What this means is that thought goes right on even when there is no self, no thinker, and no self-consciousness. Thus there is no such thing as a totally silent mind—unless, of course, the mind or brain (which I view as synonymous) is physically dead. Certainly something remains when the mind dies, but this "something" has nothing to do with our notions or experiences of a mind, thought, or even consciousness.

What I call a "silent mind," then, is a purely relative experience belonging to a self-conscious state wherein silence is relative to its absence, its opposite, or to some degree of mental quietude. But in a fully established non-relative state—which is non-experiential by ordinary standards—there are no longer the variations, degrees, or fluctuations that could be known as a silent mind. This does not mean we cannot pass beyond the mind to "that" which remains when consciousness falls away, but it does mean that whatever lies beyond has no such tool for its description.

One way to look at this journey is to see it as a process of acclimating to an unselfconscious mind, or as a transition from a relative to a non-relative way of knowing. But however we care to regard it, the fact remains that the initial, most noteworthy effect of the falling away (or cessation) of the reflexive mechanism, is a silent mind. This means that the silent aspect of the mind is actually the absence of self, or as I prefer to call it—the silence of no-self.

Ordinarily it never occurs to the mind how completely subjective it is, or how automatically and unconsciously every thought, word, and deed is filtered through a self-conscious mechanism. Thus, when the door upon self is closed, we seem at first to be in an unusual dimension; but because everything appears as usual—or because life goes on as before—we are at a loss to say what has changed. We know something is missing but cannot put a finger on it. When this happens, or when the subject can no longer see itself, it feels lost to itself and begins groping around for some object of mind to fill the old need. Yet of itself and by its own efforts the objectless mind is powerless to do this, nor will any other object come into view or arise to take its place.

It would seem then, there is a step beyond no-self which is the objectless, subjectless seeing of what Is; and each of these steps, namely, coming upon no-self, and the eventual seeing of what Is, has a type of silence peculiar to itself. It is these two types of silence—especially the former—I would like to focus on, because they are like no other types of silence I had come upon, or could hold on to, prior to this journey.

To start with, it may be helpful to draw a comparison between man's basic mental structure and that of a dry sponge, which is light and airy and can easily be carried by the breezes that come its way. Now, if we take the sponge and saturate it in the waters of selfhood, it becomes heavy, ponderous and bloated; and because it cannot respond to the breezes, it virtually goes nowhere. If, however, the sponge can stay away from these waters and no longer allow itself to be used, it will eventually, by sitting alone and aloof for a long time, dry out and return to its original structure. But there's another way this can happen. This is for an outside agent to pick up the sponge and squeeze it dry—quickly and all at once—and then put it aside to be used for other purposes than the absorbing of water.

The sponge that has been quickly dried has, at first, a unique sense of lightness, emptiness and freedom. It takes a while to adjust to a new way of life wherein it eventually discovers that the basic structure of the mind and its faculties remain intact and perfectly functional, but functional in a new way, a way no longer weighed down by the absorption of water. Although it knows there has been some radical change that seems to be a transformation into something other than what it was, in time it sees it has only returned to what it was originally; and thus, everything seems to be the same as before, with the only difference being the absence of the waters of self.

If we could fully realize how every cell of the mind is saturated with the waters of self continually oozing outward (projecting) and seeping inward (absorbing), we might have some idea of what it would be like if all such movements came to an end. Once the mind can no longer reflect on itself, all energy or movement of self is gone; the feelings and emotions are in silence; the memory has been so denuded that the past is lifeless, with no continuum at all. From here on, each small event becomes the totality of the moment, and when this moment is over, it too has no continuum. Introspection becomes impossible; and projection is also out of the question since we can no longer endow any object with its usual values, meanings, and purposes; nor can we touch upon objects when there is no water forthcoming to go outward.

Our ordinary frames of reference have disappeared leaving an empty mind, and since the mind can hang onto nothing, it must remain in the darkness of its own un-understanding. Initially it is not only the thinking powers of the mind that are silent, but it is every cell of the sponge that has been wrung out and must wait in emptiness for the breezes that will carry it along. Here we have encountered a mysterious, unique type of silence; and since it is not of the self, it is as nothing ever experienced before. In truth, it is the permanent silence of no-self.

Some people think that silencing the mind or the continual flow of thought is what it takes to be rid of self. Perhaps Descartes would think so; if he can say, "I think, therefore I am," it would also make sense to say, "If I don't think, therefore I am not." In reality, however, non-thinking produces mere nothingness, whereas a silent mind is not a blank mind. Rather, it is a mind in which the reflex arc—or whatever it is that allows the mind to become an object to itself—has been broken in two or ceased to function, so that thinking goes right on, but now bypasses the synaptic self that continually colors incoming data before sending it out again. When this break occurs, it naturally eliminates a great deal of thought and thinking, but only that which was constricting and irrelevant in the first place. As said before, the thoughts that now come to mind do not arise from within, but from the outside or "off the top," so to speak, and then, only when dealing with the obvious data at hand at any given moment.

Initially, it seems that "doing" replaces thought because when we listen, talk, read, or work, we are (at first, at least) accompanied by a mysterious silence, which is nothing more than the relative absence of a functioning self-conscious mechanism. In this way the mind is always clear, but not clear of thought per se, only clear of thought that had been clouded and infected by the waters of self.

Once I had come upon the silence of no-self I recognized it as a coming together of various types of silence I had experienced earlier in life. As a way of clarifying this state and making it more recognizable, I would like to recount several of these experiences, because at some time or other, everyone has undoubtedly touched upon no-self.

Fleeting moments of this state occurred off and on beginning at the age of six or thereabouts. Lying in the bow of my father's boat, my body in tune with the roll of the sea and my mind absorbed in the rhythmic splash of the water, I felt I had gently and quietly dissolved, and all that remained was a small, weightless cork floating aimlessly and contentedly in a vast, endless sea. The hustle and bustle of life had come to an end, and despite the continuation of sound and motion there was a mysterious silence and stillness in the atmosphere which could not be accounted for—perhaps it was just the peace and quiet joy of the elements themselves. I could have remained this way forever … when suddenly, an arm was thrust out of the porthole with a hot dog in hand. It was a rude awakening, a gesture I could not, for a moment, understand; it appeared out of place and harsh by comparison. But of one thing I was certain: all that appeared to be, including myself, was not all there was; there was something else around that was better, and I determined then to find it.

In searching for this experience I discovered that while I could not make it happen, I could nevertheless put myself in situations conducive to its recurrence, and thus, alone and out of doors, lying on the grass, under a tree in the hills, or floating on the sea, I became acquainted with this experience, which I now recognize as fleeting moments of no-self—moments that would one day be the whole of time. In retrospect, I also understand why, at that time, those foretastes could not have become a permanent state. The ground must first be prepared so there will be no rude awakenings or contrasts between what appears and what Is; and we come to this gradually by continually readjusting our lives in order to see deeper into what exists. Indeed, it takes a lot of living before no-self can become a permanent state.

About this same age I came upon another type of silence, a silence I always referred to as my "blank mind." This was discovered while listening to the Lone Ranger on the radio—or when I finally decided the best thing about this program was its music. Whenever it was tuned up (from the Ranger's end of it) I would put my ear to the speaker to let the music empty my mind, free me from my surroundings, and drown me in its tones. Later I discovered that when I tried to concentrate on a school lesson or a difficult math problem, my mind would again gravitate to this same blank state. Finally I discovered I could "go blank" anytime I wanted to. In this way, I learned how to tune out the world and become free at will.

I found this mental silence strangely attractive, intriguing and mysterious. It seemed to exert a forcible pull downward, down into an abyss of darkness and silence that had varying degrees and levels. I used to wonder how far down it went, or if there was an end to it, and what would happen if I went all the way. On one occasion I discovered what would happen, and in so doing, met up with a frightening possibility.

I was eleven at the time, and finding myself in a boring classroom, decided to put my head down on the desk and go blank. But as soon as I did this, I knew I had sunk in further than ever before because the emptiness was so complete I seemed to lose all memory of myself. At first I tried to visualize what I was wearing that day, and when this failed, I tried to remember getting up in the morning and the faces of my parents at the breakfast table; when this couldn't be done, I tried to remember my own face, and when this proved impossible, I put my hand on my head to be sure it was still there. In doing so, I noticed my arm felt like a dead weight and realized that my physical energy had been drained by this silence which now appeared heavy and oppressive. Suddenly I was afraid I would never be able to move out of this silence again—never be able to remember myself—and with one thrust of sheer panic, I leaped out of the seat and began taking deep breaths to get back a sense of myself.

After this I vowed never to go blank again. Yet sometimes the forceful pull inwards, to drop into this unknowable silence, was so strong that I had to get up, run, or do something to divert its influence. There was

nothing spiritual about this blank mind, I never connected it with a thing except to blame it for all my stupidity,
because I was convinced it prevented me from develop-
ing a profound thinking mind. As soon as the questions
became too profound I would not only go blank, but forget the questions as well. I had a poor memory and,
seemingly, no imagination since it was impossible to retain visual pictures without mental strain.

Nevertheless, in time I lost my fear of a blank mind
and in the end, came to regard it as a blessing in disguise
that served me well throughout life. This is a type of silent mind in which self can be lost from view, and on
this journey it was this silence of no-self that became a
permanent state. It goes without saying that I could not
have lived in this state at an earlier age, the developmental process alone would not have allowed it. As
said before, there was yet a lot of living to be done.

At fifteen I discovered yet another type of silence,
a silence that was not of the mind and not that of the little cork which was at one with its environment; rather it
was a silence at the inner core of my being which I called
the "still-point." Before taking this journey I looked
upon the self as the totality of my existence—body and
soul, mind and feelings—it was everything BUT the
central axis about which it moved or revolved. Compared to everything outside this center, the still-point
appeared to be still, unmovable, permanent, silent and
utterly peaceful. It was the source of joy and great energy, and once I realized it was God, I went after it and decided to embark upon a contemplative vocation.

This type of silence can spread outward (or possibly draw inward) to engulf the faculties of mind and
emotions to such an extent that, at times, all that remains

of self appears to be the still-point Itself. But here too, the experiences were impermanent, and after two years (I was now seventeen) the still-point vanished, leaving a black bottomless hole at the center of my being. In this way I entered the Passive Night of the Spirit, a night of terrible psychological pain, a burning out of the faculties of mind and will, which lasted nine months without letup. I was fortunate, however, in having the only spiritual help I was to find in my life, a Discalced Carmelite priest that I had known for several years. His joy over this darkness seemed proportionate to my misery, for he had this theory that the lower you go, the higher you rise—"like a ball," he said. Thus, with his encouragement I sat still, grit my teeth, and took all the pain I could, hoping against all conceivable odds he was right about this whole thing. I might add that the pressure behind the eyes, spoken of during the Passageway, was also at work here; evidently it is the herald of a new type of seeing.

After this Dark Night, the type of silence I met was like the great calm after a storm. But increasingly it occurred to me that it was all too natural—as if it were part and parcel of my own being and not at all from God. Eventually this gave rise to the idea that I was nothing more than a quietist since there was nothing in this silence, only silence itself. These fears grew disturbing, until I finally met someone who assured me this silence was a grace for which I should be grateful, and that if I gave no space to these fears they would disappear— which eventually proved to be true.

This silence, however, is not a silence of the mind, but the permanent accessibility of the still-point that is now always seen—known and experienced—and into which the self can descend or dissolve through varying levels and degrees of silence. This was ever a joy and on-going refuge from the troubled waters that often surged overhead, for the still-point is a place of peace and imperturbability lying below the surface of life's events and surroundings. Though I would often wonder where my silence left off and God's began, I eventually found enough troubles in life to just be glad we were "there"—and let the devil take the rest.

This is not the place to describe the various levels of interior silence, but in passing I would say that the pattern of all transient experiences is to act as a foretaste of yet a further state that lies ahead. Thus, when we first come upon a silent mind—or any other type of silence— it is a new and unusual event, but one to which we imperceptibly adjust while the next step is being revealed. In this way, what appears transient in the beginning will gradually, in the end, become a permanent state. This explains why no two experiences are alike and why they never repeat themselves, for the surest sign of no growth is no change. This also explains how life is a continual movement, and why the contemplative is one who is aware of this movement.[2]

---

[2] I might add: while all foretastes of an advanced state (such as we experience in ecstasy, for example) appear glorious and impermanent, by the time we have actually grown into this state or reached it, it will have become our ordinary, everyday state—a fact we often forget. Thus we never recognize our present state for what it really is, and this fact keeps us humble and wondering if we have made any advancement at all. This means that our true growth in the spiritual life—which is the work of grace—is imperceptible to consciousness, and imperceptible on a daily basis. This is why I mistrust those who claim to experience constant bliss and ecstasy, for if this were their true state they wouldn't know it, it would be so ordinary and everyday.

The present journey, or second contemplative movement as I have called it, was a coming together of every type, level and degree of silence that had ever been experienced; at the same time, it was the end of all such experiences. In retrospect, it is possible to understand the nature of these silences as the stilling of self, a step-by-step movement or entry into the irreversible and permanent state of no-self. It seems that from the day we are born, or from the day self begins to develop, we are getting ready for a life without a self. It is as if the mechanisms of self-preservation and self-extinction are living in balance and guiding us to our true destiny. And if the former predominates in the first half of life, it is the latter that comes to fore in the second half where no-self becomes the true, preserving force.

What this means is that all our experiences of silence are nothing more, yet nothing less, than the silence of no-self—a mysterious foretaste of what is yet to be. It means that the waters of self are gradually being wrung from the structure of being; that the mechanism of consciousness is coming to an end in a way we may never understand. Above all, it means that without a self we are free to come upon that which lies beyond any notion or experience of self and silence. No-self is not God; rather, it is the gap between self and God and the gateway to what is not only beyond the self, but beyond no-self as well.

The first contemplative movement then, is the transition from self to no-self, while the second movement is the transition from no-self to nowhere—meaning nowhere in particular, yet everywhere in general. It is a transition from the relative silence of self to the non-relative silence of what Is, and if I call the latter a silence it is because no words can be used for Its description. It can be known, however, known as it knows Itself, for what Is knows not words, nor does it communicate as such.

Once the journey was ended I discovered the increasing ability to sustain more fully the great intensity without the light going out—that is, without going unconscious, blacking out, or dropping into an unknowable nothingness. Thus there came the necessary strength to bear the vision with full knowing—seeing. In doing so, the awareness of everything else falls away—body, surroundings, silence, everything—and compared to this intensity, the loss of self is as nothing, for man and the whole universe has far more to lose than itself.

The step beyond no-self is like the dissolution of *that* which remains when It draws back into Itself as if overcome by Its own intensity. Even though what Is is all that Is, its acts or doing—which is identical with Itself—is not its entirely, for what we ordinarily know of It, is only that which falls into the realm of the known—the created, that is. But there seems to exist a fullness of act that does not fall into the known or created, and to be overcome by this fullness means that at any moment, all we know to exist may easily, instantly and painlessly, be dissolved into what Is. I do not understand this mechanism, but I do know this dissolution, this enduring intensity, is the ending and the last of all silences.

Part II

A Closer Look

Questions and Comments

After several friends read this account, I realized the necessity of clarifying certain aspects of the journey's events. For one person, at least, the complaint referred to gaps in the transition between one phase of the journey and another. To give an example of this, I was asked what explanation I could give for the seeing of Oneness suddenly turning into the seeing of nothingness. At the time, of course, I had no explanation—which was half the problem—and even now I can only conjecture that it was part and parcel of the transition from a relative to a non-relative type of knowing. It seems I had been given time to see how every sensory object faded into the same identical Oneness, before it became necessary to see Oneness directly and immediately, without going through the medium of sensory objects or individual form. As long as we can still see Oneness through the medium of sensory objects (that is, the created world), we continue to live and perceive on a relative plane, which means we are still able to see no Oneness or its opposite—such as the horrible void I saw on the beach. In other words, as long as we see God through the created world—as Oneness or even a formless "something"—we are still on a relative plane and therefore just as likely to come upon no God or no such object. Why? Because in the end, God will be seen without the medium of either the senses or the relative mind—our subject-object type of knowing—which *is* self or consciousness.

What this means is that prior to the Great Passageway and with the help of the 3D glasses, I was still able to switch back and forth from a relative to a non-relative type of knowing, or to see Oneness as well as the multiplicity of this world. Once beyond the passageway, however, there was no seeing of either Oneness or multiplicity, only the seeing of what Is, which is beyond the relative plane and, therefore, beyond even the One and the many. Thus on a strictly non-relative plane, what Is is the Eye seeing itself and wherever it looks it sees only Itself and nothing else.

* * *

Another point to clarify is that the seeing of nothingness is not the seeing of world-as-illusion. For me, nothingness and illusion have no relationship; in fact, I am not sure what an illusion is because I doubt I have ever seen one. My own notion of illusion is that it is merely an error in perception which, I now see in retrospect, goes on as long as self colors the world as something it is not. Compared to a non-relative reality, all our thoughts about the real are illusions of a sort, but until we "see," we have no way of knowing this, and therefore have no way of recognizing an illusion. Once beyond self we see our illusions or errors in retrospect and realize they were only what we *thought* about reality, thoughts that had nothing to do with the real world of objects and forms as they are in themselves. I see the world and its content as utterly real, even though they have no individual existence of their own, but are totally dependent on the One Great Reality—the One Existent. At the same time, I recognize that all form is fragile, subject to change, and that it may easily and quickly dissolve into the Oneness from which it came; but none of this is an illusion. Nevertheless, I think I may know where the notion of world-as-illusion came from or where it originates on an experiential basis.

By the end of the journey there is no longer the sensory ability to focus on the particular or individual, because the state of knowing is such that what Is becomes the only reality seen everywhere. It is almost like looking at the world through a veil so that objects are no longer clearly defined. This is a reversal of the type of perception given by the 3D glasses where sensory form gave way to Oneness; because here, at the end of the journey, Oneness is seen first, before it gives way to form. Consequently the veil grows thicker every day, and the distinctness of form grows proportionately dim and faded. But I figure the day I can no longer see anything through the veil, or see anything else but Oneness—when there is no form left to see—I too will be gone, dissolved, as all form will, into Eternal Form or what Is. In the meantime, I cannot regard the continual coming and going of my children as the interruptions of mere illusion—though I admit it would be helpful, at times, if this were true.

* * *

Another point that arose in the course of the reading was the impression that I was often in a daze of unreality, a dream-like state, perhaps, or a state of bewilderment and confusion. Such, however, was not the case; no one suspected anything unusual going on, and had I told them, they would not have understood anyway. A religious friend said he was amazed when he read the account because he had no idea, despite our frequent discussions, that anything of this nature or intensity was in the process. There were no personality changes, no illnesses, and apart from a number of memory failures, no atypical behaviors. In a word, no one judged me to be anything but my usual self. To account for this, I can only say that the preparation must have been right: by temperament, an extreme realist; by profession, a mother; by the grace of God, a contemplative; put together, these somehow got me through. But more important perhaps, from earliest childhood I was familiar with the ways of God and never doubted these events were of His doing. Even at the end of the Passageway, when confronted with the rock-bottom, absolute nothingness of existence, I was convinced that this truth had led me to this end because, for me, truth and God were synonymous. I trusted this truth, however it cared to reveal itself at any given moment.

But if, on a practical level there was no mental confusion, on the impractical or intellectual level, I was indeed surprised and bewildered by events I did not understand. Yet, when the mind lives solely in the now-moment—which is akin to a state of unknowing—it becomes incapable of disorder and confusion, for the now-moment deals only with the real, the actual and the practical. In contrast, it is the continuous, unsettled movements of the mind in a state of knowing that are solely capable of giving rise to indecision, confusion, unreality, and so on.

* * *

When it comes to maintaining psychic balance on a journey of this nature, time is yet another important factor. It would be impossible to acclimate in a single day to the falling away of self. Beyond self lies a whole new dimension of existence, a change so radical that it requires a revamping of every aspect of our life—mind, feelings, senses, on down to physical sensations. Apart from certain time lapses, I was not impressed with any sense of timelessness unless, of course, this means living without clock and calendar, which I did in the mountains; this proved interesting, but nothing more. If anything, I was impressed that this change took time— years, in fact—and that time itself seems to be the essence of life's movement. I cannot say the ultimate reality is timeless, I can only say it has its own time. This factor then, may have been responsible for the ability to take the journey in stride since the now-moment moves forward imperceptibly, but dynamically nonetheless.

* * *

In some ways, the fact I always appeared so completely ordinary may have worked to my disadvantage when, on occasion, I went in search of help and found that no one could take me seriously. I wasn't a monk or a nun; I didn't "practice" a thing; I had no charisma and exuded no light; I was just a woman geared to a teenage milieu—in short, I inspired no one. According to one Zen monk, the reason I had to have a self was because I was not omniscient and omnipresent. Since this is the Christian notion of God, I thought he was joking and laughed heartily, only to discover he was in earnest, because this is indeed the Buddhist notion of someone who no longer has a self! Evidently I was in the wrong camp—but how did he know? I think he was only telling me I was just too unspectacular, too ordinary, and too common to have come upon no-self.

This reply was in keeping with another comment made by a friend who said that for her, at least, the ending of the journey was a letdown; after all the sound and fury, the final seeing was so ordinary and unspectacular it was difficult to appreciate by comparison. I could understand this comment, after all, how many can honestly appreciate the triumph of being common and ordinary? Who can understand what it means to learn that the ultimate reality is not a passing moment of bliss, not a fleeting vision or transfiguration, not some ineffable, extraordinary experience or phenomenon, but instead, is as close as our eyes, as simple as a smile, and as clear as the identity of "that" which remains when there is no self? The expectation of the grand finale being one of love and bliss is a failure to realize that such responses are the responses of self to its own experiences, while what Is does not respond to itself in any similar fashion. On the contrary, it can be said that the Eye sees itself as "usual," just as it "ordinarily" does all the time, and is a "common" sight wherever it looks. If we had been looking at ourselves all our lives, at what point would we go into ecstasy upon seeing ourselves? It may only be deceiving to think the ultimate reality is love and bliss since such experiences may have nothing to do with God at all. As said before, I am convinced we continually see this Reality all our lives but do not recognize it because it is so usual, common, and ordinary that we go off in search of more tantalizing experiences—experiences more gratifying to the self. Thus, when we can look in the mirror and not experience the great disappointment, but can say instead, "everything is as usual and nothing has changed" then, perhaps, we shall know the intense triumph of being common.

* * *

Another comment concerned the notion of "doing," which a friend thought could easily be construed as a need to keep busy, occupied, or even, becoming a workaholic. Though I hope this impression was not conveyed, I see the need for clarification if "doing" is thought to mean the changing from a contemplative to a more altruistic or active way of life—which are compatible, if not identical, ways of living already. For a better understanding, it might be helpful to contrast the notion of "doing" to John of the Cross' notion of the "perfect act," which is an act undertaken by anyone who has attained the state of union with God. In this case, such an act is a perfect act of love no matter what the act is in itself. It could be a prayer, a household chore, or a sharing and concern for others. It is a doing for the sake of love and prompted by energies created by a union that must find expression in an outward flow. At the close of the first or earlier contemplative journey, I came upon this type of energy and act, but it is not the same act or doing I speak of here.

In the present movement there are no such energies anymore—no experience of any energy at all. Thus there is nothing within to go out, nor is there anything without to reach for. There is no longer even a union of love because when there is no self, there is nothing left to be united. Here it is discovered that God is a unity whose acts cannot be divided or separated from his existence. Thus from here on, to act without a doer is to do so unconsciously, because it is your very nature to act and you cannot do otherwise. Where self had been the will or energy formerly experienced—the doer, in other words—here there is no self to get into the act. But without self or a doer, act or doing goes right on because it is identical with existence. Another way to understanding doing is that it takes the place of the will. Since the will *is* self, and the seat of all experiential energies, and since it is now gone, how is it possible to live without a will? The answer is that "doing" takes its place; thus "doing" goes on even without a will.

The notion of doing is difficult to convey because we usually think of it in terms of a doer, of doing "something," or of "what" we do; but all this is the content of doing and is a divisive factor we are not ordinarily aware of until there is no self. But when there is no longer any separation between act and being, then and only then, is there "doing." It is not easy to get used to doing without a doer; indeed, the very thought of it is unthinkable. Yet the body functions this way all the time. No one is telling the heart to beat or how their liver must function. So who is doing this, who is in charge here? We call this the "wisdom of the body," which is a good example of doing without a doer.

* * *

Purely on the surface, there is a certain similarity between the first and second contemplative movements. Some twenty-five years ago I wrote about the first journey, and in looking over my notes I noticed that the final chapter was entitled "Doing, not Being"—obviously, still a division between doing and being—in which there was an overwhelming need to vent the energies created by a newly revealed oneness with God. But before coming upon the need for doing—at the end of the first journey, that is—I had undergone a severe Dark Night and a loss of self (dissimilar from the present journey) that seemed, for a time, to culminate in a dead-end, when suddenly, something burst in and I "see." At the end of the first journey I saw how God was Eternal Movement and that I must follow if I were not to thwart the burning force encountered by a love I could not contain. It was a love that wanted to move outward either to give to others in the marketplace, find creative expression or, if nothing else, become a test of endurance—which was the path I was destined to take.

Despite these similarities, however, the end was not the same because the journey was not the same. In the early years there had been the struggle between nature and grace that eventually disappeared into a powerful sense of wholeness that had to move outward, because now the energies of self were in tune with the Eternal Movement. While the second journey also ended in unity, it was a different unity, the unity of "that" which remains when there is no union, no self, and no God for the self. Here, no energies are forthcoming to go outward; instead, there only remains the intensity of act (doing), the act of sheer living, the living of a nature so intelligent as to be incomprehensible and inaccessible to the mind.[3]

I regard the second movement as a continuation and completion of the first, and look upon the intervening years in the marketplace as the test of endurance or necessary proving-ground, before the second journey can become a reality. There is a tendency to confuse these two movements of the contemplative life. They not only have different beginnings and endings, but what comes before and after the unitive state differs greatly from what comes before and after the falling away of self. It is thought that God as he is in *ourself* and God as he is in *himself* [4] is merely a difference of theological concern, whereas each of these is actually the culmination of two different—but continuous—movements. I think the reason for this misunderstanding is due to

---

[3] There is a great difference between the union of God and self, and the immanent unity of God beyond all creation and self. Also, there is a great difference between the union of Uncreated and created energy (self), and Uncreated energy as it exists solely in itself. What self experiences is created energy, whereas Uncreated energy is non-experiential.

[4] While I dislike using reflexive pronouns for God—as well as gender, neuter, and relative pronouns—the fact is, man developed his language around himself and not God. This is why contemplative experiences are difficult to articulate and why their language is often misunderstood. On the other hand, since God does not talk or have a language, man's lack of a language for God may only be a reflection of God.

the inadequacy of the accounts recorded, or because these accounts were not sufficiently personal or detailed to fill the gap between theory and practice. The second movement is not well known or understood, and the reason may not be difficult to surmise.

To journey beyond self means leaving behind not only our relative notions, expectations, and theories concerning what lies beyond the known, it also means leaving behind all our previous experiences, be they spiritual, mystical, or otherwise. It means going beyond our usual frames of reference and encountering areas of theological sensitivity which, alone, might necessitate such accounts remaining unrecorded or unpreserved. I have always been of the opinion that John of the Cross, with the Spanish Inquisition breathing down his neck, failed to give us the full story. We know that his writings were left incomplete.

* * *

In keeping with this I was asked why, with the falling away of my Christian contemplative frame of reference, I did not seek help from other religious or philosophical traditions? The answer is that I did, indeed, search for other life preservers, but I was never destined to make the right contact—if such even existed. I was not familiar with the Eastern disciplines and found their paradigms and terminologies quite foreign. I could never get hold of their notion of reincarnation, karma, illusion and so on; nor could I ever have had their own understanding of self or Atman. Though I doubt any of this would have been useful to me in the past, it was too late now. It may sound easy to change directions in midstream, but I do not see how it is possible after going this far. When we hit the rapids is not the time to step out and study the structure or soundness of various life-preservers that may or may not tame the stream for us. Furthermore, it seems the very nature of the crossing is an unhinging of every idea or belief we cling to regarding the structure of the world, self, and God; an unhinging for which there are no substitutes, no life-preservers, and no changing in midstream.

If I had any life-preserver at all it was nature itself, for in the most dire moments of total void, the fantastic design of my peacock friend was set up as the toughest contradiction to an unknowing mind. Every morning as we ate our cereal—often from the same bowl—I knew that although every intellectual and theological expectation had been smashed against the rocks of a reality they could not penetrate, the plumage of this friend by my side stood in opposition to all notions of void or chance. But the simple and obvious evidence of an ingenious artist at work could not penetrate my mind because I could not "see" and knew I couldn't. Thus, faced with this intense contradiction, I sometimes put down the bowl for him to finish and turned away. In other words, I saw, but could not see.

Early in the journey, while reading a book by Thomas Merton, a Christian contemplative monk, I came across the Buddhist's notion of no-self and followed up this important discovery by reading several books in this philosophical frame of reference. Reading books, however, will never lend verification for an experience outside their own frame of reference. Thus, to seek more understanding and clarification, I spent a week at a Zen Monastery where I told them, in all honesty, I had come to find out how I might ascertain—according to their own tradition—if I had any self left or not. I also asked them to please explain to me what remained when self was gone. My questions must have seemed naive to them for the silence I met seemed to indicate these questions were a monastic taboo. There was no discussion, no explanation, no answers, and consequently, no help.

Once again I was forced back upon my own resources, which were growing scantier every day. In all fairness, however, I admit to meeting a similar silence when, shortly before this journey began, I sent a note to my Hermit friends on the Big Sur telling them I would give a dollar to any monk who could tell me where self left off and God began. Needless to say, I didn't lose a penny because there wasn't a single take. Without a doubt, when her time comes, every woman must go it alone.

Perhaps the only philosophy or theology that can help us cross the stream is one that admits: when you have learned it all and lived it thoroughly, then you had better get ready to have it all collapse when you discover the highest wisdom is that you know nothing. It is said that St. Thomas Aquinas, after writing his masterful tomes on Christian theology, suddenly had an experience of God that so silenced his mind that ever after, he never wrote a single word. In fact, he said that everything he had written was "straw." Thus even St. Thomas literally fell outside his own frame of reference when he came upon "that" which no mind can comprehend nor pen describe. But now we are all stuck with these tomes, tomes that cannot enable us to see what he saw, and to which we cannot cling if we are to do so. It seems that ultimately we must go beyond all frames of reference when the cloud of unknowing descends, and all the thrashing around looking for life-preservers won't do a bit of good.

Nevertheless, I now see a possible line of travel that may be of use before crossing the stream. It would be to start with the Christian experience of self's union with God whereby we lose the fear of ever becoming lost—since we can only get lost in God. This is done with the help of Christ, the ever-present guru or master who, unlike other mediums, is always around when you need Him, both in the stillness within and in the silence of the Eucharist without. But when the self disappears forever into this Great Void, we come upon the Buddhist discovery of no-self, and learn how to live without anything we could possibly call a self, and without a frame of reference, as we come upon the essential Oneness of all that is. After this we come to the peak of Hindu discovery, namely: the identity of the One Ultimate Existent that is all that Is—All, of course, but the self.

I am not a scholar of religion East or West, and though I know each religion feels it can ford the stream alone, I think it far superior to ford it together, because it is a difficult stream to cross no matter how well the life-preservers are constructed. Theoretically, such an eclectic approach may be impossible, but after taking this journey, I am convinced that on an experiential level, the pivotal truth of our major religions ultimately come together. This, at least, seems to be the way the stream flows.

* * *

Finally, I would briefly comment on a statement made by an individual who was incensed at my calling this a "contemplative" journey, because from her point of view it was nothing more than a psychotic head-trip. Since I am not a psychologist, and apart from the fact that I could find nothing comparable to this journey in the psychiatric literature available to me, I have no rebuttal to offer this particular perspective. Meeting up with an unknown horror, memory lapses, loss of self and other events, are not, for that matter, outside the classic contemplative literature. What I could not find in either literature, however, was a completely sane, religious, comprehensible, step-by-step account of a total, irreversible loss of self, followed by a period of acclimating to a totally new dimension of existence. Nevertheless, the view of this journey as a psychotic event is not truly disturbing because, for some, this view may be all they know.

But what remains inconceivable is that having been a contemplative all my life, I should have suddenly fallen outside God's plan for me or outside his control. That the contemplative often walks the fine line, dangles over pits, and touches upon unusual dimensions of psyche and soul, is all part of this great adventure, part of coming upon the truth of God as he exists beyond all self. Those who go strictly by the books are only living vicariously. Those who call a halt at dogma and sentiment, or when the going becomes psychologically uncertain or frightening, are probably not true contemplatives to begin with. But whatever my ignorance of psychology, as a contemplative I have done my homework and am familiar with the literature in this, my field of interest. For this reason I know that the permanent loss of self is a step in the contemplative life, but one that has had little coverage. Later I shall give my reason for saying this.

* * *

Earlier, I gauged the end of the journey to be a time when the relative difference between life with or without a self was no longer apparent. I would carry this further to include all relative aspects of the journey such as seeing, doing, the silent mind, and so on. These were learning devices within the acclimating process that eventually out-wore their usefulness once the newness of discovery had been sufficiently incorporated into an ordinary way of life. Though no longer of practical use, I wrote about these because they belong to this transition or acclimating period, which was—and I underscore—a *relative experience*; merely a journey from an old to a new life.

While it was in progress, I never thought of this as a journey or a transition *per se*; instead, the basic conviction was that of having to acclimate to a profound, irreversible change in one whole dimension of knowing, seeing and being in this world. Yet it was a change that, in the end, became most ordinary in itself. This period in the contemplative life is not easy to articulate and, possibly, this is one reason it has been lost to the records, which is no help for those who come upon this step and wonder why no one has said anything about it. We will always have with us those who speak to us from the "other side," but what we really need to know is what they went through, personally, to get there.

Since everyone knows how to get as far as the stream (the subject of most contemplative literature), and since heaven (the other side) can take care of itself, what we need to know is something about the crossing itself. We need to articulate, describe, understand and explore the passage as best we can, because even if it will not help the man in midstream, at least he will know such a transition exists, and will not expect to wake up some morning to find himself on the opposite shore fully adjusted to a new life—as if by some miracle. The only person I know who showed us this crossing by his personal example—and not by his words or descriptions—was the man who ended his life on the cross. Christ did not go out in a state of bliss because this isn't the way it happens; this isn't the road to the resurrection—to a new life. That it would take such a complete death to the self, even the greatest of selves is, as I see it, Christ's realistic message to all who would cross the stream.

* * *

When returning the manuscript, a friend asked me, "Now really, would you honestly recommend this journey to others?" I had to laugh, her use of the word "recommend" made the account sound like a sales pitch for a travel agency, wherein I was recommending everyone buy a ticket for what, to my friend at least, was a most uncomfortable journey. As it stands, of course, the choice to make this passage or not to make it, is not ours. When it is time for departure—a time no man knows—

this ship of life moves into new waters, and without a self, we have no say and no control. Then too, starting from different directions, we will each pass through a different terrain and set of events. We will each be going beyond a different self and thus, the relative differences we notice along the way will not be the same; no two journeys can possibly be alike.

On the other hand, the word "recommend" is not terribly invalid, especially if we ask ourselves if Christ would recommend that we too be crucified; or, if we too are called to go to such lengths of selflessness in order to "see." Our answer will naturally depend upon the light in which we interpret Christ's death: did he give up his self so the rest of us would not have to do so? Or did he give up his self to show us the lengths to which we must go in order to see?

Since it is not within my ability to explore the theological aspects of some possible answers, in the next chapter I will, nevertheless, give the answer I came upon at the end of the Passageway. For now, I will only say: yes, I would recommend this journey; not mine, of course, but any man's journey that would allow him to see "that" which lies beyond everything we can call "self."

Where is Christ?

Of those who read this account, one person regarded it as a Buddhist-type experience, another called it "pure Vedantic," while others saw it variously as an existential crisis, a middle-age syndrome and, in one case, a complete enigma. What struck me as curious, however, was that no one suggested it was a Christian experience, which from beginning to end, was and is the only possible view I could have of it.

I look upon it as that part of the Christian contemplative movement that found its ultimate resolve in no-self and the "seeing" already discussed. Little has been written about this movement beyond self; so little in fact that my search only recently came upon several pages in Thomas Merton's *New Seeds of Contemplation* (pp. 282-285), which seems to refer to it. For the most part, it seems contemplative authors take for granted that the more advanced soul goes no further when its interior life bursts into a flame of love, and remains that way for the rest of its life—as if this were the end. Actually, it is only another beginning.

When I asked a religious friend why he thought no one had seen this account in a more Christian light, he told me the Christian influence was not obvious because there were no references to scripture or to the teachings of the Church. I had, by my own acknowledgment, fallen outside the traditional frame of reference, or the beaten path of mystical theology so well traveled by Christian contemplatives. In a word, what happened to that hallmark of Christian revelation: where is Christ?

My immediate response to this question was a complete silence. But my second response is this: if understood correctly, the answer to this question is the key to the entire journey. If I had had any assured answer to this question from the beginning, I do not see why I would have taken this journey in the first place. I was continually asking myself: what remains when there is no self? Who or what sees Oneness? Could God be the stillness within? Could he be the terrible Taskmaster? And why, in the absence of self, had nothing moved in to take its place? As an answer, Christ was not self-evident. God was not self-evident. Nothing was self-evident. This was a journey to the unknown, which is why it was so incomprehensible and why I bother to write about it. But yes, indeed, I too wanted to know: where is Christ?

Off and on during the journey, I wrote about Christ because I felt I was beginning to see him in a totally new light—beginning, perhaps, to see as he had seen. Still, this notion lent no certitude. I could make no claim of duplicating his personal experiences when, in fact, I didn't know them, and all I could do was surmise. Nevertheless, I felt this certitude might be the clue to the entire journey and the final solution as well; and in this, I was ultimately not mistaken. It was not until the end of the Passageway, however, that any sort of identification could be made, and it is this identification I would now like to discuss. But first I would like to clear up two points in particular.

The first point regards a frame of reference. As I see it a reference is only as much as we know about any system of thought—in this case, religious thought. That which remains unknown or remains to *be* known, *that* to which all religions point, falls outside the system itself—as happens when faith shifts to seeing. In some way, everyone's experience of God falls outside a systematic way of knowing, because the experience itself is beyond that. I have often thought of Christ as one who fell outside his Jewish frame of reference when he saw its truth and went about setting the record straight. He had fulfilled the scriptures (done it all), realized its truth, and set out to open the eyes of others—those still within this frame of reference. Basically then, a reference is for those who do not see. With the onset of seeing, however, the frame of reference is seen in a totally new light wherein the old light pales by comparison, and in some areas, is seen as no longer applicable.

It is this possibility that makes the contemplative's path somewhat dangerous: he is continually beset by the fear of "falling out," abandoning too much, or being so honest with God, himself, and others, that he might possibly get thrown out. It's much easier to stay with the known, cling to our references, remain put, and go nowhere. On the other hand, there are those who, from the outset, reject any and all frames of reference and these too, go nowhere. There is a difference, however, between those who reject a system and those who eventually see the truth in it. But either way, man can get lost, because this is the risk for those who accept or reject alike—but then, what is life without its risks?

I might add that it would be wholly misleading for someone who had crossed the stream to tell others that because all paths come to an end at the water's edge, they must therefore reject any and every path they believe in. Certainly this is a premature and faulty insight. Since such a person denounces the very path he took himself, he unwittingly cuts himself off from those who come after—those he might wish to help. It is as if such a man had been handed a precious gift and told that if he used it wisely, he would obtain his greatest desire. Having used the gift and attained his objective, however, he buries it instead of passing it along. Such an individual has somehow failed to see that the path that brought him to the stream is the same one that continues unseen and unrecognized over the waters. It is the same path or gift that had promised him a safe crossing in the first place. Everyone must make a beginning on some path, one he believes will get him to the other shore when his time comes. This belief, this path or gift, is not nullified when the other side is reached, or when belief finally yields to seeing.

The second point I wish to make refers to the absence of scriptural quotations. I think it is obvious that this account was not *apropos* to the use of scripture. Like everyone else, of course, I could have made use of quotations, but then, to what purpose? This is not a mystical treatise; I am not a theologian, a mystic, or an official representative of the Church. What is more, if there is anything in this account contrary to scripture, I would not know how to respond.

Earlier in life, the Bible was often a source of con-
solation and insight; at times, it described my experiences better than I could have done myself. Nevertheless,
the events in the present movement were more of an
apocalyptic adventure for which I had no mind at all.
Like Job, I had only to endure and wait, because neither
history nor specific words had any meaning to me. But
more important perhaps, is the fact that the emphasis in
my life was never on scripture; rather, it was on God's
on-going presence, revelation, communication and interior direction in the here and now. That this interior life
eventually fell away was only for the purpose of entering a larger stream of life, a stream that took its own
course wherein the search for direction is no longer of
any avail. On this journey God no longer speaks or com-
municates as such; it seems his final word is "Be still,
and see that I am God."

Returning now to the question "Where is Christ?"
I think it is important to give some background before
proceeding to give the answer I came upon at the end of
the Passageway. The reason for this background is to
show how this question had a precedence in my life
long before the journey began. Though baptized before
I breathed and once again after—just to be sure—and
given the best Catholic education in home and school, I
was nevertheless destined to have a struggle with
Christ, a struggle of long duration wherein I continually
sought a resolution that ever eluded any form of finality.

This struggle began with a playground incident
when I was ten or eleven. At that time the recess "rage"
was dodge-ball, but because I was on crutches I could
not dodge. Yet I could throw so well that the final shots

were always handed to me. Thus it turned out that every day the best two dodgers were left in the ring, and every day I hit them out. Then one day after a game, when the bell was about to ring, these two girls, who were also sisters, came to me and said:

"You think you're hot stuff because your father is rich. Well, we've got news for you. Christ said it would be harder for a rich man to get into heaven than for a camel to get through the eye of a needle! He also said that the beggar Lazarus went to heaven and the rich man went to hell ..."

"Yeah," said her sister, "Christ loves the poor the most, you read the Gospels and you'll see ... he was poor himself, and he said it was the poor who would inherit the kingdom of heaven..."

"He also said you can't serve two masters at once," added the first sister. "You can't be rich and love God too ... he came for the poor, not the rich ..."

I don't remember what else they said, but initially I wanted to assure them my dad owed money to Barker Brothers Furniture Store and that we were not rich. But they didn't give me a chance. The bell had rung and everybody was lining up, all I got in was the last word:

"I'll tell you one thing," I said, "I'd rather be rich and humble about it, than poor and proud of it—like you guys—because the proud aren't getting to heaven either!"

All that afternoon I occupied myself in class thinking up rebuttals with which to slay my friends after school. But the more I thought about the issues they brought up, the angrier I became because I realized everything they had said was true. Christ had, in fact, come to save the poor, the oppressed, the sick and the sinner, but since I was none of these things, how had he come for me? And what about others—my parents to name two—who were not poor, didn't suffer, and had never sinned? Why did Christ die for us, what was his special message to us? When I couldn't think of any answers I decided to go to church after school and ask Christ directly.

The church was adjacent to school. To the right of the altar was a life-size crucifix from which Christ looked down with sorrowful glass eyes on anyone standing beneath. Under this gaze I asked my questions, but barely got them out before a sense of some unknown tragedy swept over me like a wave that washed away my questions as if they didn't count, as if they were meaningless, childish. It was not a sense of pity or sorrow, but a sense of tragedy so profound as to be inexpressible and totally un-understandable. Suddenly it occurred to me that maybe nobody really understood his death or even his message, and it was this, not his physical suffering, that was the real tragedy: nobody understood him! Though I wanted badly to understand what evidently had not been mentioned in the books, nothing came; the tragedy was impenetrable. I felt the door of my understanding was closed.

Finally I decided I had been taken in by a pair of glass eyes and moved backward until I touched the pews behind me. But the eyes followed, intently watching as if through their eyelids. To avoid this gaze I went to the other side of the church, but here too the eyes were still watching. I found this exceedingly strange, even frightening, and thinking it might only be my imagination, I decided to move to the rear of the church, since I knew that if the eyes were still looking, I could not possibly see them from such a distance—it was a very large church. This proved correct and I finally felt free to ask my questions. After doing so, I let my mind go blank to be sure the answers would be his and not mine—but then, I had no answers so there was no fear on this score.

An hour must have gone by while I paced back and forth across the rear of the church. No answers came; only a stubborn silence, a veritable blank wall. I grew impatient, surely these were not tough questions for God; he had all the answers, so why would he keep this one from me?

Finally, at one point it occurred to me: the reason he didn't answer was because there *was* no answer. He couldn't tell me why he had come for me because he hadn't come for me at all! Many are called, but few are chosen, and I was not among the few. Once again I was overtaken by a wave of profound tragedy—he had in fact answered me from the beginning, only I had not understood. Now I realized this was not his tragedy, but my own, all mine—I had not been chosen! For a moment I was as stunned and horrified as if I'd been thrown out of heaven. The sense of being utterly lost was indescribable. For a moment I thought I was about to be snuffed out, when there arose in me a powerful burst of anger and outrage I could hardly contain. Immediately I left the church, making sure to slam the huge door behind me.

For the first three blocks all I could think of was how to break this news to the family, since I knew I would never go back to church again. I didn't belong; to go would be pure hypocrisy, and if they forced me, I might turn into a pharisee. My father's ire would be hard to bear, but going back to church would be worse than anything I could think of. In conscience, I couldn't do it.

When I got to the fourth block the scenery changed. The street was lined with trees, and glancing up I saw clouds overhead. At the sight of my old friends I almost cried I was so happy to see them. Nature, always so faithful, beautiful, and uplifting, always above the problems of life and always "there" to help me! I stood awhile, looking up, to let its mysterious detachment come over me, dissolve my problems and restore a lost peace. For a moment I was reminded of an experience I had a year before when the family had gone to the high Sierras for a picnic.

While the others went for a hike, I roamed the forest on my crutches and eventually managed to climb atop a high boulder. For a fleeting moment the surroundings gave way to an unknown immensity, a magnificence that had no description; invisible yet "seen," formless yet "something," unlocalized yet "there." In its utter transcendence it seemed not to notice me, and did not touch me in any way; it seemed only to be passing by. I was too stunned to feel anything and had been given no time to think, but once it passed, I felt a leap of joy that took me by surprise and instantly I knew what I had seen: it was God—finally I had seen him! I had no doubts, not then, not ever; but the joy could not be contained. It spread over the boulder, tumbled into the stream below, overflowed its banks and climbed the trees to the sky. It was an experience of a lifetime. Just its remembrance, and everything else in life would fall away as if it were nothing, absolutely nothing.

Though God had passed, the joy remained. I had only to look inside to see its traces, yet I tried not to look because I felt toward it a certain skepticism. With its sudden appearance in the mountains I recognized this leap-of-joy as an old friend that had deserted me in my illness the year before. It had refused to help me, in fact it disappeared before my very eyes, and when this happened, I was so devastated even God could not have helped me. That time the sea had to cure me. For this reason I never wanted to depend on its mysterious presence, for if things got tough, it might only disappear again. But ignore it, I could not. Despite my caution, it not only persisted, but I soon discovered it was a good detector of God's passing-by. Without warning, as if to signal, it would suddenly leap, and I would dash out-of-doors to catch the traces of a great Immensity that had already passed by.

So standing there looking skyward on this day of tragedy and anger, I thought to myself: since I've already seen God in the woods, who needs Christ? I can love God without him—despite him. In fact, I don't need him at all! Then there rose in me a great determination to love God, a determination proportionate to the necessity of doing so without Christ. He wouldn't help me, so I would go it alone. With this idea I found much peace, even joy, and continued on my way.

After dinner that night I decided to break the news to my father. Starting with the playground incident, I told him what I had learned in church, and ended by saying that despite all his fine desires, despite his having chosen for me, I was nevertheless not Christ's choice and saw no way we could force his hand in this matter—after all, man proposes, but God disposes.

I need not recount my father's credentials, but will only say that in matters of religion, few people were as knowledgeable. He knew as much about the Church, its theology and teachings as any priest—in some areas even more. Added to this was a legal and philosophical mind that thrived in a milieu of discussion and debate. He would often say that a Christian who did not ask questions wasn't worth his salt, and that an unexamined life was not worth living. When angry he could be quite dogmatic, but in discussion he was always fair and never once undermined my thinking powers; instead, he would have me push them to their limits. So this night began a series of discussions that would only end with his death many years later.

The first item he went over was the various ways in which the notion of being "chosen" could be construed in a theological context. The next item, original sin, was to become a continuing thorn of contention and discussion which I will not go into. But this night he left me with the challenge of trying to think up a better way to solve the problem of evil which, for the moment, I could not do. This led us to the redemption and meaning of Christ's life and death, followed by a discussion on the true meaning of poverty, where we hit a complete impasse. He said poverty only had merit if deliberately chosen out of love for God; I said many people had no choice in this matter and could merit by accepting it out of love for God. His rebuttal was based on the parable of the talents in which mere acceptance was not enough; somehow, a talent given had to be doubled in return. Since this was purely an economic perspective, I couldn't buy it.

At any rate, the story ends with my going to church as usual, but only after he had given me to ponder Pascal's Wager: "what if?" and "just in case!" At school the next day I said nothing to my friends. Though I wondered why they stood on the sidelines and did not play, I didn't ask. As far as I was concerned, their case was closed; but thanks to them, my case as a Christian was now wide open.

Because of our on-going discussions I soon understood my faith rested on an intellectual assent, and that the underpinnings of the Church were its rational foundations. I came to assume that any crack in this edifice and a man could be left dangling. For this reason I eventually found it more beneficial to study Greek philosophy than theology; in this way too, I could avoid thinking about Christ on other than rational grounds— cold grounds, to be sure, but solid nonetheless. Still, in the back of my mind there ever lurked the possibility this might not be the whole story, and that for me, at least, Christ could have an entirely different meaning. I continually put this notion aside, however, because if such a meaning existed, the door of my understanding was as closed as it was on the day this possibility first arose—that tragic day in church.

In the meantime, my father was taking a course in navigation in order to use his boat in the Coast Guard Auxiliary during the war. This course entailed a series of lectures at the Planetarium to which I went along as his eager companion and a born star-gazer. The following year he took me to spend a week-end on Mount Wilson where we could see the reality of a sky no planetarium can project. Here I was overwhelmed—the stars, the mountains, and the reclusive life of the astronomer, this was it! Investigating the cosmos far from the problems of the world, this was where I belonged, this was my true vocation. To this end I often attended the Saturday afternoon lectures at the Planetarium, and by the time I was fifteen, never missed these pleasant afternoons. One such afternoon turned into a momentous occasion that marked the first of two major turning points in my life.

In the middle of Dr. Muellar's lecture there came the familiar leap, and immediately I felt caught between two loves. I held to my seat almost stubbornly until I realized God had not passed this time, but seemed to linger instead. The thought he might notice me, glance in my direction, was electrifying; after all, I had a lot of questions to ask. At the top of my list was the exact identification of this "leap" within, and its true relationship to God.

Though I had been taught that God was present in all things, the *experience* of this presence was somewhat of a problem, one I had been chasing down from the age of five. Whenever I questioned my father about these experiences he basically denied that man could experience God as He was in Himself. God was the cause, a special grace to be sure, but the effects were our own. As a child I believed him and took my unusual experiences for some mysterious aspect of myself—alone. But over a period of time this conviction grew less convincing. By watching carefully, I discerned that my feelings, emotions, thoughts—everything about me—were quite separate and apart from something else that could leap and spread joy at some of the most inopportune moments. In itself it had a magnetic drawing-power which could not be ignored and, sometimes, not resisted. If I only knew for certain this was God, I knew it would change my life, because it would be the completion of a puzzle, the end of my search, and a key to the mystery of my life.

For this reason, when God seemed to linger a moment I quickly asked: what is this in me that recognizes you? The answer I received can be explained, but not demonstrated; it was more than an understanding or a certitude, it was a type of seeing I would only recognize as such later on. I simply saw a unique coming together of the God without and the God within, the same identical cause, but a cause that gave rise to different manifestations which, in turn, gave rise to different experiences. It was as if each manifestation had its own accompanying experience. But however this worked, I now knew that *God who passed by was also the God that remained,* and with this news I was jubilant. I wanted to shout "hooray!" and think I might have said something aloud because the man next to me went "shh!"

Naturally I couldn't sit still with this. The lecture was now meaningless, I had to get outside and share this joy with my friends—the hills, the sky, and all the animals. Now I understood why I loved them so much and what they had been trying to tell me all along. We were the same, we were one—all of us, vessels of God!

I'm afraid I stepped on a lot of toes making my way to the exit of the darkened room. Once outside the lecture hall, I raced across the rotunda and out into the bright sunlight where I felt as if I had suddenly been struck blind, for the pain in my eyes was excruciating. I had to sit for a long time with my head in my hands before I could look squintingly out on the hillside. On doing so, I was disappointed at first because everything looked so much the same. But never mind, I now had the key to all this marvel, a marvel to which I too belonged. There was so much to think about, I decided that instead of taking the bus, I would walk the miles home. Then too, I wanted to be out of doors to share this joy with my friends along the way.

Immediately following this insight there came weeks of a terrible restlessness, which, at first, I could hardly formulate to myself. Something was still missing. After a while I discovered what it was, and felt it imperative to get one more answer from God. I had to find out where I, personally, fit into this whole thing. God on the inside, God on the outside, but what about me? What was I worth to God? Was I (and all nature included) merely a vessel, a disposable showcase, here today and gone tomorrow? What, if any, is the relationship of the vessel to its content? The thought that there was no permanent connection caused a terrible sense of emptiness, as if I counted for absolutely nothing. To be left out of Christ's plan had been tragic and outrageous, but to be left out of this greater plan was so bewildering, the very thought of it would leave me as energyless as if the bottom had fallen out of life. This awful sensation left no doubt there was something wrong, there was something more I needed to understand, and for the first time, I began to pray in earnest. The answer to this question was crucial, more so than any other I had asked for in my life—God must let me have it!

Since I had little time to pray during the day, one evening I decided to pray all night. There was a crucifix on the wall of my room, and kneeling before it, I determined not to get up until I had an answer. Now I do not remember how I prayed, but I was always quite verbal with the petitions—which were more like arguments than prayers. I was also generous with the vows, and by this time had made so many, I couldn't keep track of them; but they were becoming useless anyway. Beyond a certain point there was no turning back, even if I had wanted to. Something in me was always forging ahead, it was all I could do to keep up with it, and right now it threatened to go on without me.

I had not prayed very long when a dart of light—like a bolt of lightning—came down from somewhere behind the wall, passed through the figure of Christ on the cross, and entered me with such force that I fell over backwards. In this brilliance, nothing was more obvious than the Trinity. There, at the beginning of a line of light was God without, the Creator and Father; and here (in me), at the end of the line was God within, the Holy Spirit and leap of joy; but midway in the path of light, and between the two, was Christ. Instantly I wanted to know: what was Christ doing in the Trinity? Though I had probably blessed myself a million times, I had never thought about him in this way—or seen him in this light. I began going through my repertory of explanations: God-man, redeemer, mediator, exemplar ... everything I could think of, but none of them satisfying. His presence in the Trinity was something else, and I couldn't put my finger on it. In the meantime, my original question had been forgotten. Instead, I put my mind to work on this question of Christ's meaning in the Trinity and how he fit into the great plan of God I was beginning to discover.

I stayed up thinking about this until I could stretch my mind no further and then went to bed, but not to sleep. I tossed and turned until almost morning when, finally, I felt myself relaxing, beginning to drift ... then the answer came and woke me up. Christ's position in the Trinity stood for everyman and his relationship to God. His relationship was to be our relationship, and his place in the Trinity, our destiny as well. His humanity was the vessel, the meeting place where God within and without had fruition and became One, so that everything created and uncreated was united and One. To know this same fruition as Christ had known it in himself, the vessel must become perfect as he was perfect. Christ was the medium through which the vessel (me) could become one with its content (God).

I never had to think about this for a minute, I knew exactly what to do next. I jumped out of bed, got dressed, and under the street lights and early morning fog, walked to church to make my peace with Christ. Later I came home, gave away all my clothes and sold my books, because now, I had to follow.

It didn't take long, however, to realize my struggles with Christ were not over, but in some respects, were just beginning. Before long I found myself in the company of those whose sentiments and devotions to the historical Christ had no precedence in myself. I had no head for mental images and was never granted a single experience of God in which the historical Christ was object. It was as if he refused to be an object to my mind and emotions however hard I tried to make this possible. Instead, he was the medium turning my gaze, not upon himself, but upon the still-point within. At first this was disconcerting and once again, I felt left out. The path of the saints has always had Christ as the object of its meditations, insights, visions, and experiences; in this I could find no exceptions. Yet, for myself, I could make none of these things happen, it was like trying to beat against a stone wall. I had to learn the hard way the futility of my own desires in this matter.

But how then, was I to identify with Christ in the reality of the here and now? Without a doubt, if it hadn't been for the Eucharist I would surely have lost track of Christ again. But in the Eucharist, Christ's presence was as invisible and formless as his grace and work in me. Thus it became my lifeline to the Trinity, drawing me into its silence and giving me the certitude that here, I had finally come home; this was where I belonged; and accordingly, I took my place.

This then, is how I came upon a middle way of traveling the contemplative life. Like a stream, I made my way between the high peaks of the rational on the one side, and the mystical peaks of extraordinary experience on the other. The stream did not climb upward, but ever coursed downward in search of its own level, its ultimate destiny in still waters. This is not a transcendent path because the stream stays low and clings to the earth, escaping none of the turbulence in the ordinary flow of life. Still, it's a dangerous course. Because the terrain is ever changing it is impossible to chart the path ahead of time, and thus without direction, I often had no idea where I was going or how it would all end. Sometimes I was carried along against my will and even with fear by a movement not of myself. Learning not to struggle against the current was, for ten years, my particular contemplative journey, until one day, the stream disappeared and traveled underground for many miles and many years before once more emerging to see the light. Only this time, the light would cast no shadow because now there would be no object (self) in its path.

While taking this first journey I never forgot the tragic eyes that followed me that day in church. I often pondered the possibility they presented: that Christ's death might have a significance other than those traditionally assigned to it. But since this was only an intuition without a counterpart in my understanding, I continually pushed it aside. That it waited almost forty years for a resolution is something else to ponder, yet it became a reality on this second journey, the journey beyond self, when the door of my understanding gave way to reveal a lost dimension of Christ, a dimension I would never have imagined possible.

In this present movement, Christ literally exploded in a crisis that would efface him totally, but at the same time, reveal him in a new and different way. One by one, the Trinity vanished. First came the loss of self, the vessel and medium—Christ; next came the loss of God within or the still-point—the Holy Spirit; and finally, the loss of God without—the transcendent Father or Eye seeing Itself. But with each loss came a compensating insight. With the loss of self, Christ dissolved into the still-point, they were One, and all that seemed to remain of this human experience. Then suddenly this too disappeared or dissolved into the One God seen everywhere. But after nine months this Oneness also disappeared and there remained only a terrible void. This void can be compared to the death of God, a crucifixion unknown by our psychological standards. It is a state of complete (non-relative) unknowing because there is nothing known to which it can be compared. In short, this void is not only beyond knowing, but beyond unknowing as well.

I have called this great void and state of unknowing a "Passageway." It was during this time, when doing my utmost to acclimate or get used to such a predicament, that a distant voice broke through the silence. I had been walking on a secluded road and stopped to look around at my old friends—the hills, trees, and wild grasses, now so empty and void; it was a look of complete unbelievability. How could I have been so duped, hoodwinked—and all my life! It was impossible ... yet, it had to be, there was nothing there. Then, above the trees I heard a distant voice asking his father why he had abandoned him, and with that, the door of my understanding began to give way.

I had never associated the Dark Nights with Christ's death. The falling away of the ego-center (Passive Night of the Spirit) never struck me as the true nature of Christ's death. Though the ensuing revelation of the "true self," hidden and united with God in the divine center, seemed like a resurrection of sorts, I never took it for the true nature of Christ's resurrection. For me, this never solved the mystery of Christ. But here in this void of voids—beyond self, union, and a divine center—I understood this man and knew exactly where he was at. Never in history has a holy man, saint, or sage of any religion gone out of this world with such a question on his lips, or ended his life on such a note. This was indeed the death of God, and a sign of contradiction to the end. No-self is a meaningless state, but no-God is an incomprehensible condition, yet a condition with which I could now identify and understand completely.

That he too had come to this end, this nothingness beyond all we can possibly call self, was strangely comforting. Here we were, companions in a great mistake, allies even in the void. I was glad I had gone as far as he had, and did not blame him for bringing me to this end. I wanted to see the same truth he had seen, and if this was it—if there was no God—then this was the end of the road. There were no regrets.

Christ had expected a resurrection just as I had expected to "see," but obviously it hadn't happened. Instead of glory, we had seen nothing; nothing perhaps, but the futility of our lives and even the pointlessness of our deaths. Yet coming upon him unexpectedly in the Passageway, I knew a closer identity with him for having been mistaken than I had ever known during all the years I thought he had been right. Now I understood the real tragedy—his and my own. It was the tragedy of all those who had believed in him, but would never come this far and would never understand a thing like this.

I was glad his loved ones had seen him after his death, at least in their own minds and hearts; after all, life must go on whether there's any truth in it or not. Someone had to stretch the human limits to find out if there was any truth beyond self, any life beyond this one, or any God beyond belief. Christ could do no more because there is no more a man can possibly do—and what man has done as much? What is more, he did it not only for himself, but that others would not be afraid when their time came to stretch these same human limits. Now I knew and understood how one could go this far, and because I entertained no hope of going beyond Christ's own ending, I turned to face the great reality—the reality of absolute nothingness.

Shortly after this turning point, or point of enforced acceptance, I did in fact "see." And when I finally saw "that" which remains when there is no self, I knew that Christ too had seen "that" which remained—a seeing or knowing that **is** the resurrection. That he never truly relinquished his certitude of eventually seeing, no one knows for sure; I think he did, because human certitude must eventually yield to seeing when God as he is in *ourself* yields to God as he is in *Himself*. Spanning this gap between human and divine knowing is a perilous transition; it is the ultimate void to be crossed if we are to enter into the fullness of divine life. For Christ, it might have been made in a split second—or better still, three days. For myself, it took almost four months.

The particular type of seeing I refer to as the resurrection is the revelation of God—more specifically the Logos—as it exists beyond the human medium of self or consciousness. It is God's knowing, and no longer our knowing—or unknowing. During his lifetime and on the cross, Christ referred to his Father in the objective sense as the One who sent him, gave him power, whose work he did and whose will he followed. At the same time, he referred to his Oneness and union with the Father without claiming absolute identity—that is, he made no claim to be the Father, or even, to be God. The statement "I am God" would not have been true anyway, because it refers to self (I, me, myself) whereas divine knowing is beyond all such references and purely human way-of-knowing and experiencing. If prior to his death and resurrection Christ's knowing was totally divine, we would not be able to explain his subjective references to God in the objective mode, nor why he had to be resurrected when he lived in a resurrected state already. Had there been nothing human about him, this would be explainable; but then, his life and death would not have been a reality.

Though the human Jesus knew God in a subjective way as being inseparable from himself, this knowing is highly analogous to the knowledge of our own union with God. When God is revealed as the divine center of our self we can truly say that God *is* our deepest, truest self. After all, if God's existence did not underlie and sustain our own, we could not exist at all. So how, then, in his humanity, was Christ's knowledge of this union different than our own? As I see it, the main difference is that in the incarnation Jesus was born directly into the unitive state; born with this knowledge from the beginning, while the rest of us only come gradually to the unitive state—and then, by way of a difficult and painful Dark Night. It is only after this, the first contemplative movement, that we meet up with the human Christ and share his own subjective knowledge of oneness with God. In this unitive state we identify with Christ in the words of Paul, "No longer I, but Christ lives in me." Thus our true self is hidden with Christ in God, inseparably one with God *through* Christ. Yet beyond this union there still lies death and resurrection, and not just for Christ, but for ourselves; for after coming to this union, nothing again can ever separate us from Christ. So the rule of thumb is this: as it went for Christ, so it goes for us.

Christ's death was the foregoing of his human self and its particular union with God—that is, self's knowing and experience of oneness with God. This is more than giving up self, it is the giving up of self's whole experience of oneness with God. Because self is the human medium by which man knows and experiences

God, the falling away of self is equally the falling away of its experience of God. Though it is not inappropriate to call this event the "death of God," the only thing that can die or cease to be is something created and non-eternal in the first place. God, of course, does not die; rather it is the purely human way of knowing and experiencing God that dies. The resurrection that follows is the revelation of the divine Christ or Logos as the *true nature* of man's oneness with God. This oneness is *not* then—as we may have thought—God's oneness with self or consciousness, intellect or will, or any such faculties of the soul. Rather, our oneness with God IS Christ and only Christ. The resurrection, then, is the Truth of Christ: the Truth that only the divine Christ (Logos) is eternally one with God, and not our personal individual selves. While this is truly the good news of Christ, for some people, at least, this seems to be too frightening to even consider.

A much overlooked revelation of Christ is that his own journey was a revelation of our own, or everyman's journey. Thus how it went for Christ is how it goes for all men. If we want to understand our own journey and what comes next, we need only to look to Christ. In this way our life parallels his own in that our first movement is coming to Christ's same union and oneness with God—God as He is in our self; and the second movement: the falling away of this union and coming upon God as He is in Himself—the Logos or divine Christ. Thus like Christ and with Christ we too must die, and not just physically, but psychologically and ontologically. For some this may seem like a hard saying, yet as I know it, this revelation or truth IS the resurrection.

That Christ knew the second movement—the falling away of the purely human medium of knowing and experiencing oneness with God—and entered the gap between the human and the divine, or between two different dimensions of knowing and experiencing, is the true mystery of Christ's death. Spanning this gap entails a descent into hell, a great void, and a state of absolute unknowing. Yet this is the passageway to the resurrection—the revelation of the Logos or divine Christ. Evidently not even a divine self, or a self that is one with God can avoid making this transition or entering the gap between God as he is in our self, and God as he exists in Himself.

For all this, however, I do not regard the resurrection as the final step; for just as it was not the final step for Christ, so it is not the final step for us. Following the resurrection is the Ascension, the final dissolution into the fullness and glory of the Godhead. With the dissolution of Christ's human form—seemingly into air or a cloud—Christ suddenly becomes everywhere. No longer limited to a single form, Christ is the One Eternal Form from which all multiple forms arise and into which they ultimately dissolve. Solely in his divinity Christ is the Eternal Form of the Formless Father, and just as Christ dwells in the Father, so his creating (or Forming) Spirit dwells in Christ.

At the end of the journey then, the earlier seeing of the Trinity—which began my journey as a teenager—had undergone a great change. Where initially Christ's humanity had stood for my self and all creation—"saving" us, as it were—here now, Christ's divinity or Logos was void of all self and all created individual form, because in the end, all created form is transformed, divin-

ized, or "transubstantiated" into the One Eternal Form.
Where at the beginning, Christ's *created humanity* had
been the "vessel" or intermediary between God within
(Spirit) and God without (Transcendent Father), now
Christ's *uncreated divinity* (Logos) is the Eternal Form or
"Vessel" that dwells in the Formless Father, while the
Creative (Forming) Spirit dwells in the Vessel. The difference is that the earlier or initial revelation of the Godhead had been according to the human medium of
knowing (self or consciousness), while the final revelation is according to God's own knowing. This is why the
passage from one dimension of knowing to another
must eradicate all previous knowing and experiences of
God—which were totally human. There is a great difference between these dimensions, and what makes the
shift possible is the shift from God in and with self, to
God beyond and without self.

I am as convinced today as I was momentarily
convinced as a child, that the real tragedy of Christ's
death is that so few understand it. The general interpretation is that Christ gave up his self so the rest of us
would not have to do so. He did it, so now the rest of us
are free. That we should have a liberated self when
Christ (in the resurrection) has no self, makes no sense.
Self is not our true life or our eternal nature; it is but a
temporary mechanism useful for a particular way of
knowing, and in some ways, equivalent to our notion of
original sin. Self may not be sin, but certainly it is the
cause of sin, and what needs to be overcome is not the
effects, but the cause itself. To be forgiven is not
enough; eventually there must be an end to the very
need to be forgiven.

Christ did not overcome our individual self for us; he only showed us by his death what we too will have to go through to be truly free, not merely free of sin, but free in the most divine sense. Christ not only mediates this overcoming of self, but in the end is "that" which goes beyond the self to endure the passage and finally see. If the truth be known, when self's transformation into Christ is complete, it is *only* Christ who dies and Christ who rises. For some people this is a hard saying, but as Christ said, "Let those who can take it, take it!"

As emphasized before, the bewildering aspect of this journey was the failure to recognize "that" which remained when there was no self. The stillness within was just that and nothing more, no one, nothing, appeared to take its place. Continually I was expecting the divine to reveal itself within, but it never happened; obviously the final seeing was not to be of this nature. Here I think of how Christ's loved ones also failed to recognize him after his resurrection, because without a self, Christ cannot be recognized in this fashion any longer. Thus he had to reveal himself all over again in a totally new and different light. Not the light of belief, but the light of disbelief, since what is seen ever remains unbelievable to the thinking mind. Indeed, it is because Truth is unbelievable that man needs faith—faith, which is beyond belief. To say that "God is all that is," the One Absolute Existence, is not only unthinkable and unbelievable, but to some, it is absolute blasphemy. Our minds cannot comprehend this; it must be seen to be believed, and yet once *seen*, it is no longer believed. In this way, belief or our frame of reference eventually gives way to seeing.

If I had never had a self, I would not be able to understand why man clings so tenaciously to the certitude of its permanence. Whoever was responsible for the idea of dividing the self into lower and higher parts committed a serious crime against humanity. This division has given rise to the notion that the lower (ego and immature) self must be overcome while the higher (unitive and whole) self must be sought as the goal of human realization. Out of ignorance, I too had clung to this notion because I believed it was this higher or true self that would be united with God for all eternity. It took a long time before my experiences led me to doubt this conviction and, at the same time, let in the possibility that this was not the whole truth and that there was still further to go.

It was in moments before this second journey began, when overcome by what lies beyond all self, I learned something was yet wanting; there was still another step, this was not the end. I intuited a far greater and more final surrender that made me afraid at times; but the day this fear disappeared was the day self disappeared and the journey began. Before this happens, however, I am convinced that one's trust in God, the great Unknown, must be tried in fire, otherwise this fear remains and will never be overcome. The final relinquishing of self (the higher unitive self) may therefore constitute the only true act of faith in God man can make; while clinging to God, our union and experiences of Him, may be a great mistrust and the ultimate expression of disbelief.

At one time I believed self was necessary in order to love God, for if "I" didn't (or we didn't), who would? This was the reason of our birth and the meaning of our lives: to love God. But shortly before this journey, I discovered that self does not love God at all, because "that" which loves God in ourselves is God himself. To say it is "I" who loves is to unwittingly deflect selfward and claim for the self what belongs to God alone. Only God is love, and for this love to be fully realized, self must step aside. And not only do we not need a self to love God, but for the same reason we do not need a mind to know him; for that in us which knows God, is God.

Before crossing over the line to the Unknown—and becoming unknown myself—I had been given to understand that from now on, it would be God loving Himself not *in* me, but *in* Himself. I found this confusing and wrote pages on the issue. I was already convinced it was not I who loved, because the love I experienced was already beyond the self; rather, it was Christ in me who loved the Father—or God loving Himself—but still, it was in *me*. Perhaps it was the Holy Spirit loving the Father in Christ and not in me ... I finally gave up on this enigma saying: I do not fully understand, and let it go at that. Two years and an unusual journey later, I did understand. It meant that God would no longer be loved in me, but solely in Himself; and no longer known by self, but known with his very own knowing. But how this works or what it is like is beyond any possible formulation or communication.

It is one step, and a giant one, to see clearly and participate in the love that flows between the persons of the Trinity, but even here, God is seen as the object of his own love. It is yet another step to realize that God is beyond all subject and object and is Himself love without subject or object. This is the step beyond our highest experiences of love and union, a step in which self is not around to divide, separate, objectify, or claim anything for itself. Self does not know God; it cannot love him, and from beginning to end has never done so. Anyone who has experienced this love surely realizes that it is beyond any and all capacity of self. If this were not so, there would be no going out of self.

After this account had been written, there occurred what I call a "last experience," which resulted in an insight into the nature of Christ. I called it a "last experience" because of its similarity to the very first experience I had at the age of five. Its recurrence at this time gave a sense of closure to my life, the quest of forty-five years. Before recounting this insight, however, I will first describe the two experiences.

The earlier experience came as an overwhelming surprise. I had been on my way to play a game of cops-and-robbers when suddenly, from within, I felt a swift, powerful infusion that stopped me in my tracks. Like a balloon I seemed to be expanding in all directions, but when I looked at my arms and legs I could see no visible signs of this. Whatever this power was, for a moment I thought it might overwhelm me—squeeze me out or take over—and I had no idea what would happen then. At first I was frightened and thought to myself: I'm gonna bust! But at what seemed to be the peak of its expansion, it stopped. I held my breath in suspense, and then across my mind came the words "you're too big for yourself!" With that came an explosion of enormous joy, like a great voice laughing. After this, the power gradually subsided until everything was as usual again—though I would never to be the same. I always regarded this experience as moment I was *really* born.

At the time, I did not think of this as an experience
of God, I only knew for certain it was not myself. From
that day forward, however, I could see this mysterious
power within; it became an ever-present friend and
teacher. But after four years it suddenly vanished, and
was not seen again until I came upon God in the woods,
some eighteen months later. With the initial infusion,
however, there began the relentless quest of tracking
down the true nature of this experience, or true nature
of the power. It is because of its similarity to this first experience that I call the following a "last experience."
Here I take it from my journal.

> What I saw take place was just a possibility,
> which I experienced only briefly. It was almost
> frightening. I saw how God can invade a form,
> take over a human form. This is perhaps the most
> total loss of self possible. In this invasion there is
> power unimaginable and the only consciousness
> remaining says "I am God." There is something
> almost frightening about this type of total posses-
> sion. I saw how I do indeed have something left
> of my own. After all, my words and actions are
> my own; I know I am not the totality of God and
> there is still something left that could be done
> here. This was not an explosion outwards but an
> invasion, like a comet coming down above my
> head and moving through the whole body. It
> was a possession like the swift blowing up of a
> balloon, like the act of creation, only here, the
> form was already waiting. I don't know what to
> make of this, but I am skeptical. I do not know
> what It may do in this form—just how human is
> divine life? All this reminds me of Christ, this
> must have been his own experience. I see how

this would be so—see it clearly. Yes, he is one
with God and is God himself. At the same time,
though possessed and full of God, Christ is not
the totality of God because a man's form and faculties limit God, and yet, somehow they don't.
God is not limited by form, rather God is only
limited by our own uncomprehending minds.
Form is merely the act of THAT which never
changes and ever remains unknowable.

Anyway, I saw how this possession or invasion
works. It can be frightening. To lose yourself is
one thing, to become God is another. I think I
would just as soon stay in my present state neither totally possessed nor totally myself. It is difficult to point out the difference between "what"
remains (when there is no self) and this total possession; both are God, yet one is full of God and
neither has a self. In those moments of being possessed I felt a bit of a struggle as if not sure, not
understanding. It was all very risky, and yet I
knew there wasn't a thing I could do about it. I
had no choice. So what does all this mean? I
don't know, but what I know for sure is that God
can possess this form far more than He does at
present. He can take over and obliterate any other knowing but the one that says "I am God." I
don't know what to make of this but it's all very
interesting. Maybe it's a foretaste of some future
event. I hope not!

Later I wrote at length about this incident and concluded that for God to infuse himself into me was like
trying to blow up a balloon with a thousand pinholes.
Without a self, form is porous. Here there is no self to

capture, transform, or hold onto the divine; no self for God to overshadow, work through, or impose itself upon; nothing to which the divine could become attached. To have a divine mission, however, man needs a self—a will, a driving energy, and above all, self-consciousness—and thus Christ had to have a self to do God's work on earth. But how did he come by this self? At one time was his human self overlaid by the divine in a type of union that has enabled men to become emissaries of God—such as saints, seers, and prophets? God has always had such mediums, so in what way was Christ different? Based on the above experience, God's possession of Christ was more than a union of the human and divine, more than a type of consciousness or someone suddenly overpowered by God.

Although no-self cannot be a medium, it nevertheless stands in a unique position for such an actuality. In the absence of self, in a completely empty form unconditioned by this world and untouched by self (and sin) from the beginning, God could create and fashion a type of self unknown by our relative standards, even our highest standards of union with God. Such an admixture of the human and divine is not only incomprehensible, it would be impossible of realization at any stage of our self-becoming or union with God. Thus despite our oneness with the divine we are not, for that matter, other Christs. We cannot identify our self or any level of consciousness with the mystery God fashioned in Christ. This means that if there is any time in life we can honestly identify with Christ it is from the position of no-self, or when we have entered the gap (the void of voids) between the human and the divine. Here we can truly identify with this man on the cross who willingly gave up his self, his powers, his union with God, to show us that God lies beyond not only our usual notions of self, but even our most divine notions as well.

Until there is no self, I do not see how it is possible to have any true identity with Christ, because this ultimate identity, or no-self, is necessary if we are ever to "see." Until this point is reached God remains a love within, a power above, the other half (or objective pole) of our own subjective consciousness—however we envision God as not self. And indeed, God *is* other than our self, on the cross he is no-self. For me, at least, this is the true message and meaning of Christ, where, even more than his words, he showed us by his death what each of us will have to go through to "see," to be resurrected, to be "raised up" beyond ourselves.

In conclusion, then, the incompleteness of my understanding of Christ which began as a child was the ongoing struggle of my Christian life. Without this continual search for an honest level of identification with Christ, I would not have been Christian. What seems to be given to others at the outset was, for me, a slow revelation of painful honesty and continual questioning. It was a way of darkness and unknowing so little understood by others, I was left to forge a way and go it alone. How could I identify with Christ when I could not use my imagination? had no experience of God in which he was the object? and more often than not, found the Gospels trite from sheer repetition? Evidently his mission in my life was not to be one of fulfilling emotional or intellectual needs; rather, it was that of a mediator who never permitted himself to be an object, but diverted my gaze to the still-point instead.

I could never equate the historic Christ with the still-point, and yet the notion that he lived in some remote heaven was equally unacceptable. I could not identify with his selfhood because I knew it was of a totally different nature than my own. Much less could I identify with Christ on a symbolic level since, from earliest childhood, I could never believe in myths or fairy tales—once removed as they are from reality and truth. Christ is not a symbol of anything, but the great reality himself, and to find this reality was the quest, my life's journey.

I looked upon his historical life as over. The message remained, the grace was always there, but the man was gone. With his Ascension into heaven I felt he had dissolved into the fullness of God so that the continual effort to separate him out—be it on an imaginative, emotional, or intellectual level—was, on my part, worse than dishonest, it was a phoniness I could not live with. So how then could I identify with this incomprehensible man-God, and identify with him in truth, in the here and now?

Gradually I discovered a way. His presence in the Eucharist was mystical, his grace was mystical, and his work in me was mystical—a work done in silence and darkness. Thus to accept him on these, his own terms, I had to meet him on the same level: a mystical level that, for me, was deep, hidden, unknown, and inexpressible. Here I could identify with Christ as he gradually imparted to me his own vision of the kingdom of God—the still-point within. Because of this, it could easily be said that I never knew Christ personally—on the level of personalities, that is—and on this level, he did in fact elude me all my life. Nevertheless at the end of the present

journey, I finally confronted this man in a smile-of-rec-
ognition. And with this smile, my understanding was
complete, the struggle was over.

Christ is not the self, but that which remains when
there is no self. He is the form (the vessel) that is identical with the substance, and he is not multiple forms, but
one Eternal Form. Christ is the act, the manifestation
and extension of God that is not separate from God. We
cannot comprehend "that" which acts or "that" which
smiles, but we all know the act—the smile that is Christ
himself. Thus Christ turns out to be all that is knowable
about God, because without his acts, God could not be
known. Act itself is God's revelation and this revelation
is not separate from God, but *is* God himself. This I believe is what Christ would have us see; this is his completed message to man. But who can understand it?

Complete understanding can only come at the end
of the journey because full, complete understanding
from the beginning would nullify any necessity of taking a journey. This is why we only came upon the full
revelation of Christ at the end of the journey, and not at
the beginning. What always struck me as unusual on
this journey was that Christ seemed to followed me, and
not the other way around. It was only *after* certain experiences, or after I had come to a certain point, that Christ
was revealed, but not during or beforehand. By coming
"after," however, Christ verified what had been lived
through and shed light on its underlying reality—his
own Truth. It seems that nothing can be truly verified
or honestly understood until it has first been lived,
which is why the Christian journey is a lived reality and
not merely an intellectual belief. In the end, then,
Christ's mystery and revelation only unfolds as much as

we ourselves unfold; and if grace precedes, revelation follows.

This, at least, was my Christian life, with its on-going quest for an honest, absolutely truthful, final identification with Christ. For me, God-transcendent (the Father beyond creation and self) was never a problem or a mystery, nor was God-imminent (the Holy Spirit in creation and self). The problem was only Christ, and this mystery, more than anything else, is what kept the journey going. Belief and understanding of Christ are only complete once we see, and once we see "what" Christ is, we know "where" Christ is, for these cannot be separated. Once we see how Christ is Everywhere, we realize that without Christ, the very question, "Where is Christ?" could not have arisen. Though we cannot say where God-Transcendent is (because he transcends "where"), we can say, Christ is Everywhere, because there is nowhere he is not.

Self

The usual method of studying self is to view it in relation to the collective, the other, the unconscious, or whatever is designated as not-self. My approach to this study, however, is by a different route. Because of this journey I was able to know the true nature of self solely by its absence or no-self; in other words, I learned what *was* when I learned what *Is*. Although every method of learning is by some relative means, the study of self relative to not-self yields a different set of insights, experiences, and conclusions than when it is known relative to its absence or no-self. Naturally, it is only with these latter findings that I am concerned.

Owing to this particular approach, I must leave behind the usual theories, psychological speculations, and methods of studying self, especially when these begin with the assumption that self is a permanent entity, an indelible or permanent fixture of human nature, and my point of departure was the sudden realization this was not so. It is important, I think, to point out these different perspectives because what I have to say may be incomprehensible and unacceptable to those who have taken the traditional route. In turn, I have to admit that I never understood the analytical approach or scheme of the psyche; its failure to recognize God (not the self) as the true center of being, made such an approach foreign and incomprehensible to me.

I think it is safe to begin by saying that without the reflexive ability of the mind to bend on itself, there would be no thinker of thoughts, no doer of doing, no feeler of feelings, and thus, no such thing as self. In the autonomous act of bending on itself, the first thing the mind sees or knows is itself, and without this reflexive action, the mind has no way of knowing itself. Due to this reflexive mechanism, then, the mind can only knows itself as object to itself and thus, in the realm of consciousness, the subject *is* the object. The true object of consciousness is not an object of the senses—something we can visually see, hear or touch—rather, the true object of consciousness is always and only itself. This means that what the self or subject is, is the mind knowing itself as object to itself, and this subject-object way of knowing is the true nature of consciousness. But the knowing-self is only one of the two experiential dimensions that compose the whole of consciousness. The other dimension is the feeling-self, and about this we will speak latter on.

It is important not to mistake the nature of consciousness for the nature of the sensory system. Where the reflexive mechanism enables the mind to look inward and be self-conscious, the sensory system only looks outward to respond to its environment. The difference between the sensory system and the system of consciousness is actually the difference between animal and man. A problem arises, however, when we fail to distinguish the immediate object of consciousness—self— from sensory objects in the environment—what we visually see, hear and touch. The reason we confuse one object for the other is because all incoming sensory data is filtered through the reflexive mechanism of the mind, and thus every sensory object that enters the mind bears a subjective stamp, which stamp is not the sensory object, but rather the subject itself.

So the problem is that as long as the reflexive mechanism remains functional, we may not be able to fully separate sensory objects from our self (or from the subjective stamp, that is). It is only after the permanent cessation of the reflexive mechanism that this separation becomes automatic, and the difference between the two systems—consciousness and the senses—becomes clear and obvious. Learning to live with the senses only, and without consciousness or self, however, entails a very difficult acclimation process. A process I would even categorize as an unthinkable feat.

The experience that initiated the events in this book was the permanent cessation or closing down of the reflexive mechanism of the mind. It was no longer possible to look inward or reflect, and though I strove with all possible energy to remain self-conscious, the mind kept falling into the silence of no-self or no con-sciousness. Not only had self disappeared as object to it-self, but disappeared as subject as well, for being relative to one another, there cannot be one without the other. What was obvious, however, was that some as-pect of the mind had opened onto the Unknown in a contemplative gaze, a gaze with which I was well ac-quainted, but never before so continuously enforced or permanently focused, a gaze out of which the mind could not even move. By allowing this gaze full rein (there being no other choice) I became used to the inability to look within, and in this way the senses gradually took over—became able to stay awake or to overcome the continual inclination to fall into the same void as consciousness.

Though realizing self was gone, it remained possible to force one final look inward, and on doing so, I beheld not one, but two voids. Not only was self gone, but suddenly God was gone as well—the two, after all, had been one single center. With the disappearance of the divine center it felt as if all life's energy had suddenly been drained away. What went out was a sense of life I never knew I had because it was not connected with the senses or the body's ordinary energies. This indescribable sense of life and being constitutes the other dimension of consciousness we spoke of earlier—the feeling-self. As a subtle energy, this profound sense of life is not the knowing-self, but the feeling-self located at the center of consciousness or center of being. Together these two dimensions—knowing and feeling—constitute the whole of consciousness and are responsible for everything we experience as self. The falling away of this self was not a passing experience, but an event that ushered in a whole new dimension of existence, an existence wherein there was no self anymore. This new dimension had first to be discovered, and then adjusted to—a period of many years.

In the first event, then, or closing down of the reflexive mechanism, I could no longer *remember* myself; in the second event or falling away of the divine center, I could no longer *feel* myself.[5] I believe this sequence of

---

[5] There are two steps to the falling away of self. The first is recounted in Chapter 1 of this book, and the second, in Chapter 2. The most extraordinary step is the sudden disappearance of the center of being,

events to be important because, in retrospect, it enabled me to piece together this experience called "self," an experience that seems to disappear in the reverse order of its initial appearance. And as to how the self arises, I will have something to say in a moment. After these two events and as I moved through the following weeks and months, I gradually discovered that the major result of these experiences was the disappearance of the entire affective system. It took a full year, however, before this dawned on me, and the circumstances under which it did so—the horrible void I saw on the beach—made it, initially, a hard pill to swallow. I saw myself as unwittingly trapped without a means of escape when I realized that once the self is gone, the resultant state is irreversible; the affective system could not be resurrected. In turn, this recognition was responsible for the unfelt, unknown terror and dread that afterwards came to mind. But once it had been confronted openly on the hillside, this insane phenomenon never reappeared.

It was here I discovered that the stillness of no-self would hold fast against the most terrifying and unknown machinations of the mind. I learned that without any feelings to back it up, the mind is absolutely powerless to effect a single thing. At the same time, it became obvious that the stillness and silence of no-self was, indeed, a marvelous and irreversible blessing.

Through these events I came to understand how the indefinable, personal sense of subjective energy and life was the nucleus, the tough core around which the affective system was built; a system that not only belongs

---

which is also the energy center that runs the reflexive mechanism. Self is far more than a way of knowing, above all, it is the feeling of being, life, and energy that defies experiential description.

to the self, but *is* self. The feeling of personal life is like a seed within that branches out to permeate every aspect of our being; and to be without self, means to be without this seed, this gut-level feeling of personal being, life and energy, along with all its branches, the entire affective system. In the second event of the journey then, this seed and all to which it had given rise was uprooted in one fell swoop like a tree that had suddenly been felled. Life goes on, but it is a new life, one that is neither personal nor impersonal—it is simply life without a self.

So this was what I discovered: self includes the entire affective emotional network of feelings from the most subtle unconscious stirrings of energy to the obvious extremes of passionate outbursts. Though separate from the cognitive system, the affective life so infiltrates the mind and all its processes that we can never separate our energies from the cognitive faculties as long as consciousness or self remains.

Ordinarily we do not realize the extent of this infiltration because we like to believe we can be purely objective at times, when in fact we cannot. Subjectivity and objectivity are two sides of the same coin, the same consciousness, and though the intellect remains intact when the affective system disappears, it then functions in a different way, a way that cannot be described because there seems to be no mind at all.

To account for the rise of the affective system, we need only remember that the child *feels* long before he *thinks*. It is only gradually, with the development of the reflexive mechanism, that he discovers a separation exists between the seer and the seen, and with this discovery he becomes self-conscious. And once this takes place, his feelings become inseparably fused with his knowing. Thereafter both the knowledge and the feeling of self are all but indistinguishable. When the self disappears, this knowing-feeling self disappear together like twin systems of a single circuit.

Because feeling precedes self-consciousness, it should be noted that the mere acknowledgment of self as an object of consciousness is insufficient to account for the self's existence. Without a sense of personal energy or feeling to back it up, such knowledge is so lifeless and meaningless, it is no more than a mental construct as easily dispelled as a child's belief in Santa Claus. But self is more than a knowledge of its own existence, and what this *more* is, is a gut-level feeling of energy, drive, power, and of a will that, when linked with the cognitive faculties, becomes the subjective certitude "this is me," "I am myself." This energy permeates our thoughts, words, and deeds to such an extent that we have come to believe these feelings are part and parcel of what it means to be human—a belief I now see is a great mistake. Man is more than self, more than consciousness.

Although the feeling of personal energy—which in the early years is indistinguishable from the sensation of simple *physical* energy—precedes the conscious knowledge "this is me," it is obvious that self only becomes a force when self-consciousness (which *is* the reflexive mechanism) develops to the point of claiming this physical energy for its own. Thus no matter how much physical energy man experiences, without the knowledge "this is me," physical energy has no more meaning or feeling than the noticeable effects of air and water, to which no one can make a personal claim.

When the reflexive mechanism closes down, however, the experience of both psychic and physical energy
goes with it. Though physical energy obviously remains, it cannot be experienced as before. Cut off from
consciousness, the knowledge and feeling of getting
around under our own steam is gone. At first this gives
way to a sense of weightlessness, an unusual experience
that will remain as long as any relative difference between the old way of *feeling* life and the new way of
knowing life can be noticed or recalled. As we acclimate
to a new life, the lack of feeling any energy is soon forgotten, or so I learned from experience.

In the history of the self, then, physical energy
comes first, the reflexive mechanism comes next and regards this energy as it own being. With this recognition
a division is created between physical energy and what
we will now call "self-energy," will, mental or psychic
energy, which some people believe is beyond the physical realm. Where at first there was only energy of the
body, now there is energy of the mind, which resulted
when the sense of personal energy infiltrated the cognitive system to energize its thoughts and acts. It goes
without saying that, of itself, thought has no power or
meaning unless there is some force or drive to back it
up. Rid thought of this power and thinking appears to
be no more than a neurological mechanism of the brain.
Ultimately, then, self is not only the thinker of thoughts,
but at its most subtle, rock-bottom level, self is equally
the experience of energy—the doer, so to speak.

Given this history, it should be obvious that if
someone wanted to go beyond self, it would be useless
to try and alter either the cognitive or affective systems.
As long as the brain persists with its automatic reflexive

mechanism, so long will the knowing-self remain; and so long as the experience of energy remains, so long will the feeling-self remain. Thus whatever the reflexive mechanism is, and whatever the energy that moves this mechanism, both are strategic to a life with or without self. This is why I have said that only an outside agent can bring about the demise of the self: since the reflexive mechanism is autonomous and not under conscious control, self cannot be the cause of its own undoing. To think consciousness or self can get rid of itself is a contradiction. Some day, however, we may discover the secret of the reflexive mechanism, and in doing so, we will have discovered the difference between man and beast. A premature cut-off of this mechanism could prove more damaging to human life than anything man has yet devised for its destruction.

Nevertheless, when the time is ripe—a time no man knows—this mechanism gives out, gives way to a life beyond any need of self. This does not mean we fall back into an infantile or bestial form of life. Though we continue to share in every strata of existence, the disintegration of the self is a forward, not a backward, movement. Once the mind has been appropriately conditioned to its human potential, it does not forfeit this in order to see "that" which lies beyond it.

The impermanence of self is comparable, perhaps, to the pineal body or organ in the center of the brain, which is said to be functional in the developmental years, but later ceases to function. In similar fashion, the self, which was necessary for a specific way of knowing for most of our life, ceases to function when it has outgrown its usefulness. The intervention of an outside agent has much to do with man's reaching an unknown level of psychological development—or the limit of human potential—before this agent can act, or before man can dare to live without a self. This means that self is not only our human dimension of knowing and feeling, it is also the "way" by which man eventually moves to a higher life and dimension. Obviously, then, the purpose of having a self is to eventually go beyond it.

The awareness of wholeness and unity realized before the second journey begins—which unity was made possible by self's oneness with God—is different than the Oneness that remains when there is no self. Because the experience of wholeness and unity is only relative to the experience of incompleteness and disunity, this experience is obviously relative—as are all self's experiences. But beyond self these relative experiences disappear, leaving an indescribable non-relative One. Nevertheless, it was the initial unity and wholeness that constituted the necessary preparation for the second journey; without this, I do not see how the passage could be made. To have no-self, there must first *be* a self, a whole self—a true self.

In recent years psychology has begun to explore the process of integration and the unity of self, but undoubtedly it will be a long time before it gets around to investigating the process of disintegration and the eventual falling away of self. For now, at least, I know of no one who even admits to such a possibility. Perhaps this study will come about through the efforts to extend our knowledge of the aging process or, possibly, the true nature of death. But as it stands now, it seems that self is regarded as an eternally divine necessity from birth to death and into the beyond. It is this refusal to look beyond that makes the usual study of self such a closed

system of investigation. And this refusal, like every unquestioned assumption, turns out to limit, confine, and
eventually entrap us when it leaves no door open to ontological change or to "that" which lies beyond all self or
consciousness.

* * *

Now that we have seen that the core of self is our
deepest experience of life and energy, we must go on to
say something of the branches to which this seed gives
rise: the entire affective system, which includes not only
the emotions, but feelings we do not ordinarily associate
with self. What follows is what I know of this system,
based not only upon what I discovered during the journey, but upon much that I learned before it began.

Since the affective system is on a single relative
continuum, I look upon it as a seesaw where the ends of
the board (or continuum) represent the extremes of at-
traction and repulsion, and the area closest to the near
immovable center represent its more subtle, often unconscious, movements. Supposing the fulcrum on
which this continuum rests is the cognitive system, we
can see that the process of integration is a balancing act
wherein the ultimate goal is maintaining an equilibrium
against all forces to the contrary. The greatest force acting against this balance comes from the extremities of
the continuum, while the most subtle forces, closest to
the center, are responsible for our first spontaneous
movements in either direction.

Obviously, optimum stability is achieved at the
center of the two systems, a center wherein the contemplative eventually discovers maximum access to the

still-point—which is a point not *of* the system, but discoverable through it. In fact, the contemplative's sole reason for desiring this stability or unity between systems is because the silent, quiet, near immovable center of the continuum is the gateway to the true center of his being—the divine still-point. Thus, where the equilibrium sought by the non-contemplative is only between the two systems themselves, the contemplative seeks an alignment between these systems and the still-point— once again, not to be confused with the near immovable center of the affective system.

The center of the affective system is the will, and since the will is an energy or power, the affective system takes its energy from the will. So long as the will does not move—does not want this or that—neither does the affective system move. Underlying the will, however, is the divine still-point, and thus when the will is still and quiet, it has optimum access to the still-point. This is why the desire for this and that inhibits access to the divine still-point, and why a "desireless" state is of particular value in the contemplative life. This desireless state, however, is not the end or goal, but rather the means by which the beginner has access to the still-point.

So the near immovable center of the affective continuum is the will and it is this center where the contemplative makes contact with God. It goes without saying, of course, that God is not immovable, much less a still-point; these terms are simply the language of experience and do not attempt to define God. The still-point therefore refers to that experiential unlocalized "spot" in ourselves where man runs into God. For man's part, this spot seems to be at the center of the affective continuum, which, I might add, does not appear to be dependent upon the fulcrum below (the cognitive system).

The contemplative is continually scanning this continuum looking for its stillest point, but often cannot find it. Therefore the still-point, when it can be seen, acts like a beacon on which the contemplative focuses his gaze, and in doing so, is pulled like a magnet toward this center wherein the affective system comes to a standstill. In this way, the still-point acts as the greatest inhibitor of the affective continuum that we know of; it gradually immobilizes all movements along the continuum by bringing them to rest in an undisturbable sense of peace, silence, and stillness. Above all, it rests in the certitude of Its presence.

As an inexperienced contemplative, I noticed how I often ruined this sense of presence by becoming so emotional about it that God was overshadowed and effaced by the extremes of my reactions. I knew I had to be still, but by my own efforts could not do this. When I tried to ignore this presence, to let it be, to make nothing of it, this worked better; but unfortunately it doesn't work the other way around. We can ignore God, but he can no more ignore us than he can cease to exist, and because he exists he touches us, and for this reason I made little progress in my efforts to maintain the necessary interior stillness.

It was only after the passive Night of the Spirit or unitive state, I was able to make continuous contact with the still-point without an affective overflow. The reason for this is because the nature of the unitive state is a union of wills (human with the divine) and thus a union of powers. From here on, the will can never move contrary to God, nor even contrary to the good of our neighbor, because God now holds our power of will in his hands.

The unitive state does not immobilize the will nor, consequently, the affective system. It is the movements of the will contrary to the divine center that are forever cut off or are made impossible. To discover this, however, requires situations where these contrary movements and their behaviors would otherwise arise; if not, we cannot learn how this union works, what changes have occurred, or what the unitive state is really about. This is why the marketplace—that follows the unitive state— allows maximum opportunities for these movements to arise, and why the hermit in the same state, never really understands what the unitive state is about; for him, union is the end of the line. The unitive state and marketplace, however, are only the way and the means to yet a greater end.

It was after the unitive revelation I discovered, to my relief, I could no longer experience the extremes of the continuum, because after this, nothing was able to alter the deep sense of peace, stillness and strength that the divine center provided. But if the board no longer dipped to extremes, it continued to go up and down. For years, this inner core of "all is well" was tested by a great variety of exterior forces and circumstances that tried to move the imperturbable center. At times I wondered what kept me from sliding off the deep end, but at the last minute the still-point would open up, expand, and draw everything into its silence.

So after many years in the marketplace, I knew I had unconsciously made my way to the center, or close enough that none of the responses to life's events went beyond spontaneous first movements. Because these movements were so automatic or autonomous, however, they seemed not to be under my control, and about this I was highly skeptical. I never cared for instinctual living and ever chose my head over my emotions. Then too, I had little trust in any aspect of the affective system since it never taught me the truth about anything. I knew better than to base any faith, hope or charity on how I felt that day. For these reasons I looked upon such spontaneous movements as a peculiar impasse to absolute stillness. Though harmless in themselves, I found these movements more mystifying than anything encountered before; I was not sure if they were of myself, of God, or of some unknown instinctual force. Finally I decided they represented a gap between myself and God, a mysterious dividing line or impasse I could not see my way around. But by adopting a wait-and-see attitude I was able to come to the point of watching these movements without acting on them. It was while watching that I made a curious discovery one day.

The gap between the near immovable center of the continuum and the still-point turned out to be a battleground for two opposing forces. The battle, however, was not between the affective extremes, or between the two systems themselves (affective and cognitive), but between two mysterious forces that strangely, seemed to have nothing to do with me at all. On one occasion, I had the unique experience of quietly observing this battle rage within myself without being touched in any way. Here for the first time I asked myself: who is watching this? who is this outside observer? Naturally I had no answer. When the battle dissolved, I took for granted some great issue had been settled, but having no idea what this was, I put the incident aside as yet another mystery of the contemplative life.[6]

Shortly after, I understood this battle and realized these opposing forces were the forces of self's preservation and self's extinction. These forces, however, are beyond consciousness and do not touch it; they are not under man's control or choice. At best, we can only know of their existence. The line between them is like a gate that the preserving force would close to anyone going beyond, while the force for extinction is the power that keeps the gate open. After this battle I realized the impasse had been removed; the instinctive, spontaneous first movements on the continuum were gone, and I came upon the clear possibility of making a permanent alignment with the still-point. What happened when this alignment was made is the story of this journey, a journey that not only went beyond all affective movements, but beyond the continuum itself.

In this way, the still-point gradually—over many years in the marketplace—drew this system into its silence, and once the stillness was complete, the continuum was no more, self was no more, and being relative to

---

[6] There is no way to describe the experience of this battle. It began like a quiet rumble or disturbance somewhere in the depths of my existence and lasted several days. One afternoon the battle became so fierce—seemingly decisive—I doubt I could have done anything but watch it. In observing, there came to mind the notion of two angels doing battle, where one was determined to open something up, and the other, determined to keep it closed. Initially I thought these might be the forces of good and evil, but since they did not touch or effect me, I discounted this as their true nature. I never saw the end of the battle or knew which had won out; suddenly there was an abrupt silence, a marvelous stillness. After this there was nothing to observe because these forces vanished as mysteriously as they had appeared.

these, the still-point was no more. Ultimately, then, union with God is not really complete until there is nothing left to be united; between self (the still center on the affective continuum) and God (the still-point) there is no gap remaining. What is left is what Is, all that Is, and Its identity is unmistakable.

A friend recently told me that the falling away of the affective system was invariably a psychotic symptom. While I had never heard this before and cannot verify it, my present perspective is quite the opposite. As I see it, the affective system is not only the cause of every psychological illness, it is the cause of all man's suffering. An organic problem without this system could not give way to psychological or mental suffering, because there would be no fears, anxieties, or all the rest that so easily erupt into emotional disturbances.

In keeping with this is the admission of a gentleman who said he was terrified at the thought of losing his self. What he had obviously failed to realize was that the terror and dread he felt *is* self, and that without a self there can be no such feelings. In fact, a sure sign self is gone is the absence of these affective symptoms. So as long as there is any fear of losing self, self remains—in which case there is nothing to worry about one way or the other. But this is why the histories of those who have truly gone beyond self will never be found in psychiatric literature. With no problems in the affective domain, few people would be in need of a psychiatrist or analyst, indeed, without an affective system, or without a self, this whole school of thought would be out of business.

Yet we cling to the affective system out of fear of what life would be like without it. We are afraid that without feelings we will be inhuman, cold, insensitive, robot-like creatures, so detached from this world that we might as well be dead. Needless to say, there is no truth to this view, it is just another myth created out of fear of the unknown—where all myths come from. Nevertheless, to explain what life is like without this system is basically impossible, it is a dimension that can only be lived, not one that can be understood. All that need be said is that it is a dynamic, intense state of taking care of whatever arises in the now-moment. It is a continuous waking state in which the physical organism remains sensitive, responsive, and totally unimpaired. When fully adjusted to the dimension of no self, nothing is found to be missing or wanting. It is only in the encounter with other selves that a self or affective system is a reminder of what *was*.

One reason such a dimension is difficult to imagine is that few people realize the full extent of what the affective system really is. Some people think of it as the loving heart in man, when actually this is only one side of the continuum. Its opposite, anger and hate, is responsible for the only diabolical force in existence, for I can think of no evil for which man is not responsible. Unfortunately, these affective extremes are not far apart, they are only relative to one another. A way out of this dilemma of relativity would be to live on only half the beam—the good half, that is—but it doesn't work this way; either we are potentially subject to all these movements or we are subject to none of them. Some movements, however, are so subtle we think of them (mistakenly) as cognitive or even physical, and since filtering out this system from the rest of our being is so impossible, we seek integration as a way of at least keeping it in line.

It is imperative then, to examine closely and realize that the root of the affective system is the feeling self: the feeling of personal being, energy and will. In turn, this branches out to give rise to desires and expectations that color every perception and thought, until it reaches into every experience, including the aesthetic sense of beauty, feeling of contentment, peace, boredom, tiredness, loneliness, and so on. In short, this system includes every sense of psychological interiority and feeling of contemplative spirituality that we know of.

Because the self is all this and so much more, any description of what remains when it falls away is bound to raise questions of a moral, behavioral, relational, and even, metaphysical nature. Without a self there arises the question: what becomes the standard of measurement for the good life, right action, decisions, values and so on? To say there is no standard is to say the incomprehensible, but also to say the truth—a truth, however, only applicable to no self. Before coming to this dimension, standards must exist because it is the nature of the self to create them, and then to live by them.

It is difficult to understand an effortless, choiceless condition that needs no standard to survive. The mind cannot grasp this realm of the non-relative where there is no multiplicity, union of opposites, or any need to deal with differences. This dimension is nothing more than a simple straightforward look at the One that Is, a look that can no longer scan a continuum that doesn't exist for options that do not exist. Nor does it look backward or forward because in the now-moment each moment is sufficient unto itself. It is impossible to step outside this moment wherein there is no choice and no standard.

It was this non-relative dimension I found missing when searching through the contemplative literature for insight into this particular condition. Since self is responsible for a sense of interiority, the criteria of my search was for the absence of an interior life—which, of course, I did not find. Instead, I encountered the usual descriptions of love and bliss, lights and energies, God within and the true self, all of them descriptive of the first contemplative movement, and all of them still within the relative, affective domain.

While I recognized many of these experiences, I had to discount them as belonging to the present movement. I found no one who admitted or even suggested the complete falling away of the affective life. At best, it seems that only its negative aspects are said to disappear, and it was this fact I found most questionable. If we are to live permanently at the positive affective pole, I do not see the possibility of a balanced life, nor do I see the impossibility of sooner or later experiencing a dip in the opposite direction. With the exception of the near immovable center, every point or movement on the continuum is relative to some other point or movement; thus, as long as the system exists, we can never get beyond the relativity of our experiences. Feelings of love, bliss, joy, and all things ineffable are merely relative to their opposite, their absence, or some other point along the continuum. So when I encountered these descriptions I knew they were not what I was looking for. They were not indicative of the second movement or the dimension beyond self.

It occurred to me that the falling away of the affective life might be a piece of esoteric knowledge not given to the outsider, or even to the proficient. Since he could not understand it ahead of time, as a future prospect, it could prove too frightening. So as it stands now, the high contemplative goal is generally regarded as a feeling state of uninterrupted bliss, a heavenly feeling that seems to be the accepted and expected end of man. I feel bad about this because it won't happen. Heaven is something else.

For all this it could be said, nevertheless, that so long as self remains, the affective system is a fairly sturdy tree of personal life in which every mature adult eventually feels at home. If there is any problem with this tree it is that some of its fruit is good and some of it is not so good, and as long as the tree remains productive, there is the potential for yielding either kind. This is the risk involved, the price to be paid for the knowledge that makes scientific and cultural achievements possible; but however much we are indebted to the good fruit, there is nothing eternal about this tree. In essence, self is but a temporary dimension of existence, a dimension man must eventually learn to live without; if not now, then later.

Perhaps the most relevant questions to be asked regarding the falling away of the feeling self would be the following. What takes the place of its better aspects, or how are we to account for charity, sympathy, compassion, and love? How would it be possible to regard a nonrelative dimension as "better" if it were lacking in such virtues?

For one who has made the passage, these questions do not arise because he is not aware of any absence of virtue—which does not depend on feelings, anyway. What is absent, however, is the need to practice, since there is no need to practice what is already there. What remains after the passage is not unkind, uncaring, un-understanding, condemning, or any of the rest; in short, the need to practice virtue does not arise. What before we had to strive for or put there, is now "there" of its own accord as if it were the most natural thing in the world. But if these questions are not relevant to the state itself, they will surely arise in its description, and at one point these questions were put to me in a manner I did not, at first, understand.

When handing back my account a religious friend asked me, "What I want to know is how you think this journey changed you? What were its effects? In what way are you different now?" His questions took me by surprise because, to tell the truth, I thought I had accounted for all this in the writing. I thought the changes that took place were so obvious that despite my lack of talent, the events alone had somehow told the story. With his queries, however, I saw my mistake and realized that though I should write forever, I could never make clear to others the changes that were so obvious to me. Recently someone passed on to me a Hindu saying to the effect: those who say they see, do not see, because those who see, say nothing. I can now add to this: even those who say they see, say nothing. Thus, whether we speak up or say nothing, it makes no difference.

My friend's questions, however, stuck in my mind. I was continually thinking of all the things I hadn't said—and there's quite a lot of that—but none of it apropos to his questions. Finally I decided that since he was a religious individual, he must have been referring

to the usual standard of Christian measurement: by
their fruits you shall know them. So the questions became: am I a better person—a better Christian, more
charitable, more virtuous, and so on? Although the idea
of answering "no" strikes me as particularly wicked,
this must nevertheless be my answer, because in more
ways than these even, there is nothing to show for having taken this journey. In fact there is less to see than before, because the very occasions that once arose for the
practice of virtue no longer arise. This does not imply
the absence of good, it only means that as a practice, virtue is absent. The key to understanding this lies, I believe, in the fact that the will, which provides the power
and drive to put virtue and vice into motion, has disappeared. Since virtue means "strength" or positive will-
power, without a will there is no such strength or virtue.

If it has not been underscored before, it must be
emphasized here, that the faculty of will is, itself, the
core of the feeling self and the experience of personal energy. By itself, thought is powerless to act, it must be
moved by the will if it is to have any part in our behaviors. This then, was the major discovery regarding the
self: that its very nucleus is the will or volitional faculty.[7]

Though I had often thought the will was more of a
cognitive than an affective faculty, I was never able to
place it in either category, at least experientially, since

---

[7] Looking back over the contemplative journey it is possible to trace
three moments in the life of the will. In the beginning stage, the will
is free to choose good or evil, and having chosen ultimate goodness
(God), it practices and strives for virtue in all aspects of life. But
once the unitive state is realized, the will is altered; now it is only
free to choose good because its first spontaneous movement is one of
virtue and goodness. Matters could not be otherwise since the will

the will was somehow superior and more mysterious than either thought or feeling. What I see now, however, is that the will reaches to depths that the cognitive mind cannot follow or even understand, and that it underlies the affective system as the source of its movement. When the affective system first disappears, it is not the emotions or feelings that abruptly fall away; rather, it is the very source of their power—the will—that is made immovable. As a result, the affective branches slowly fade and disappear before we even know they are gone.

Since the will *is* self, we can see how, when self permanently disappears into the still-point, the entire affective system is uprooted, forever silenced or stilled. One of the most unusual aspects of this journey is acclimating to the immobility of the will. As the source of personal energy—not physical energy—the absence of will is what causes the experience of energylessness and lifelessness that follows the disappearance of self. Much of the passage is the process of acclimating to life without this faculty and its experiences. But this may explain why, beyond the personal tree of life, there are no fruits: no virtue and no vice.

---

is now one with God's will; and too, practice ultimately gives way to spontaneous habit. But further on, with the falling away of self, the will no longer moves at all, it has quietly disappeared because it is self. Without a will there is no freedom at all; in its stead is a choiceless life. Though we are often reminded of God's free will, what possible moral choice could God have? In himself God does not know evil. We have often heard it said that God is beyond good and evil—that is, beyond man's relative choices—so in this matter, even God has no choice, no will. It may be better to speak of a divine plan rather than a divine will.

As a practical matter, however, living in the now-moment there is no question of how we feel or should feel; there is no conflict, struggle, or practice of anything, because this moment allows for no movements backward or forward, either in time or along a continuum. Somehow each moment contains within itself the appropriate action for each tiny event in life without the need for thought or feeling. This is what I called "doing," which is the ability to act in the absence of any interior experience of will or energy. It is because such a non-relative dimension is so difficult to understand that it raises many psychological, philosophical and theological questions. It is not understandable on an intellectual basis; it is beyond the logic, the theories and practices we once took for granted or thought would last forever. Apart from the immediate experience—if it can be called that—there is nothing that can be known or observed of this dimension; it cannot be seen for the looking—there is nothing to see.

I must say, nevertheless, I have always found the Christian standard of measurement somewhat questionable. Observing the fruits of others invariably relies on the subjective judgment and opinions of others, which are often more questionable in themselves than what is observed. Of those who witnessed the good works of Christ, for example, some thought he performed these works through the power of the devil, others thought his behavior insane. There was no consensus about this man; by his fruits alone, he was not known. There is a different way of knowing him, however; a hidden, personal way of understanding his identity through our own identity with God. Without this, it would be impossible to know him.

I would go further and say that when it comes to knowing others, I would not greatly trust what a person had to say about himself because words are as limited to the speaker as they are to the interpreter. This may sound skeptical, but I am convinced there is yet another way, a better way of knowing others, a way that in one sense, does not entail knowing them at all.

To understand how this works, however, it may be necessary to move beyond our usual way of knowing, move to a non-relative plane where it seems, at first, a contradiction exists. Without a self, there is also no other, and therefore no relationship. How then is it possible to know others at all? To ask it another way: how can we love our neighbor as our self when there is no self, no other, and no affective love? Before answering, I would like to explain why, for me at least, there were no changes in relationships either during or after the journey; and why this was one aspect of life that remained unaffected by stepping over the line into a new way of knowing. To do this I must first say how others were known prior to this passage, since this may be all that is really needed for an explanation.

My first intimations of a way of knowing others—apart from mere empirical appearances—occurred early in life when listening to a discussion at the dinner table one evening. My father had begun by quoting what a Jesuit had to say on child-rearing practices, in which he compared the infant to a vegetative stage of life. He did not get very far, however, before Mother interrupted. "Don't quote him to me," she said, "he didn't have any!" With that, the discussion was closed. But the conversation that followed was more interesting.

It seems that mother never mistook her babes for peas and carrots. On the contrary, she claimed she could see the Divine shining through the innocent eyes of the infant, a vision, she said, that never left once it had been seen. Now I understood this as a miraculous feat that Mother could see in me what I could not see in myself, and took for granted that one had first to be a mother before one could see this phenomenon, this vision of God in others. Later on, of course, I realized that we can only see in others what we have first seen in ourselves.

Mother's philosophy of life was based on seeing into the inner self. If I went to her complaining I was bored, had no one to play with, or whatever the childhood grievance, she would remind me never to be dependent upon anything outside myself for my happiness. Joy and contentment, she would say, are only found within and it is there we must look for it—find it. Looking outside ourselves, we might think for a while we have found it, but it won't last. For our happiness, therefore, we were not to depend upon other people, material possessions, or ever set our heart on anything to the extent we would be heartbroken if our expectations were not fulfilled. She also stressed that we must learn how to enjoy being alone and spending time by ourselves. But to live this way, she added, we must first develop our inner resources so that no matter what happened in life, we could go right on as if nothing had happened. This, then, was Mother's philosophy of life, suitable to every circumstance and propounded to us with numerous variations.

On a conscious level I never took on this way of thinking. To some extent I didn't have to because much of what she said was part of growing up. No one had to tell me I was independent, or that I had to make my way in life or find my own happiness. Yet, as I grew older, I realized what a gold mine Mother had tapped within herself, and that the real challenge of being independent was just this: tapping the inner resources. But it was due to this early perspective that I somehow—albeit unconsciously—managed to skip over the problem of relationships, because to be dependent upon others was, quite simply, beyond my expectations. Furthermore, what I learned to value in others was their independence, since it was the first thing I valued in myself.

For some individuals, however, it seems that the overriding concern or philosophy of life is that it consists of relationships, a perspective in which everything is seen as relational, interdependent, and necessary for personal survival. This view places great emphasis on the I and the not-I as being necessary for human fulfillment, and thus relationships will be the major concern—and the major problem as well. This view, however, is so foreign to me I can say little about it, but it seems obvious that if we try to complete ourselves by going out to the other (the not-I) before turning inward to the true "Other," we are making a wrong turn—a tragic mistake.

It is only when we realize our oneness with the true Other that we come upon a unity and wholeness that can withstand the test of all encounters with other selves. In this way, no matter what happens in our relations with the outside world, we are not fragmented, we do not fall apart, become lost, dependent, or see problems where there are none. It is only after we come upon the Other—the still-point at the center of our being—that we find the key to a powerful sense of security and independence that *then* allows us to go out to others, to be generous, to give them their freedom, to be open-minded and understanding. If for some reason we do not find this inner resource, we have no choice but to grasp at what is without, and it is this premature movement outward instead of inward that gives rise to all problems in relationships. The real problem in life, then, is not between people, but between the individual and his true Other.

But let us say we have found our wholeness in God, what then is our relationship with others? Since what we see and love in others is only what we see and love in ourselves, it follows that having found God within, we can now love others as we love ourselves— love in them the same Other we love in ourselves. And since love of God is beyond the affective system, so too is our love for others.

As a child, I once asked my father how it was that I felt more love for my dog than I did for God? He laughed and replied, "What you feel is called 'puppy love,' but love for God is a strong will not to offend him." Later, in discussing this emotional love versus love for God, I came to the conclusion that although the emotions may or may not be the effect of love, they are not love *per se*. Basically then, love for others is a strong will not to hurt them, as well as desiring for them the same good we desire for ourselves. Thus I was convinced at an early age that love was not an emotion, and as I moved through a lifetime of experiences, I never learned anything to the contrary.

Such a non-emotional basis of love will not be understood by everyone, yet it is easy to see how problems arise in relationships when love is based on our emotions. I have met individuals who cannot form a lasting friendship apart from emotional involvement and attachment where the other is expected to reflect like a mirror their own moods, humors, ideas, and schemes; and if the other does not respond in like manner, they go elsewhere—find someone else. Nevertheless, seeing God in others is not the same as seeing him in ourselves because, where our seeing is an immediate subjective movement inward, to see him in others we move outward to see the individual first and God second. But once seen, God is that quality in another that forever remains indefinable, untouchable, can never be possessed, or even adequately communicated.

This then was my outlook on the "other" and relationships before the journey began, and why, with the falling away of the affective system, there were no changes in personal relationships; although there was, in fact, a change in the way of knowing others. Where before I had seen the individual first, and his true Other second, now the Other is seen first—and the individual? Well, I do not really see him at all, not at least as before. Instead of a self I see ideas, behaviors, decisions, struggles, and much more, but I do not see a self because it has been paled or effaced by what is really there.

Once again, we can only see in others what we see in ourselves; so when there is no self, there is also no other. Empirically it may be true that no man is an island, but beyond this level, multiplicity ultimately fades away leaving only the One. Thus on the empirical level of differences, relations continue to exist, but exist without problems because even here, we are aware of an intrinsic bond between all that exists. Although it is veiled, a non-empirical, non-relative Oneness exists on every level we know of.

My eldest son objects to the notion that beneath the facade of individual differences we are all the same. His idea is that each individual is eternally unique despite his oneness with God. I can understand this repugnance to the notion of sameness; it somehow gives the idea that God is boring, static, without variety, and that our individual differences count for nothing. But when saying that beyond the limitations of empirical form all things are essentially the same, I am referring to God, who is the same throughout all empirical form. To realize that all form comes from the same clay does not subtract from the variety of form or its unique nature; on the contrary, the sameness and difference, the one and the many is, itself, the uniqueness and very essence of God and all that exists.

This alone tells us that the self cannot possibly account for our individuality or uniqueness. We have only to look at nature to see that the trees, the clouds, and animals do not have a self and yet are the very essence of uniqueness, variety and differentiation. Self does not constitute true individuality because this essential uniqueness remains when self is gone.

It is the underlying core of the affective system that gives rise to the subtle feeling, "my being, my life, my individuality" and so on; but without a self there are no such feelings of self possession or mistaken identity. Once we see what Is we realize: that which is different is also that which is the same. And as for the fear of losing the distinctiveness of empirical form, it takes but a single glimpse of what lies beyond this form to see that an even more unique, moving, dynamic life is but a step away. One glimpse of this new life and our present existence becomes boring, static, and insufficiently diversified by comparison. But once we see this, we are ready to move on.

Altogether then, this is what I learned about the self. Man must have a self because this is his human way of knowing and feeling—experiencing. Without it, man as we know him could neither exist nor survive. Thus self is a protective mechanism against physical death and a state of unknowing, and for a time, at least, this is the way it was meant to be. We did not fashion our humanity any more than we fashioned air and water. We are not of our own doing. We did not create consciousness: the autonomous reflexive mechanism of the mind, or the central power that runs it. We did not fashion for ourselves a free will or an affective system. It is only beyond self that human responsibility for what we *really* are becomes so small and the choices so limited, it amounts to little more than avoiding a collision with other objects. This is because without self, the sensory system obviously remains—and who can imagine the knowing to which it is privy?

Outside our choosing and doing, then, all is being moved by an unknowable intelligence, moved in one sure direction and changing as it goes, wherein the immediate goal is nothing more than the movement itself. Thus we move in and out of a variety of dimensions, different ways of knowing and being, always changing, always moving, and this movement is our delight, our revelation and our very life.

In this passage we encounter much that is beautiful and awesome, but as each step unfolds, we let go of the present and move into the new without clinging to what is passing. In the effort to go against the flow, we hold onto our insights, ideas and experiences, thinking each one is the last, only to discover we must move on, taking nothing with us, because what is essential at one time is accidental at another, and it is change that is life's movement.

At one point in this journey, self comes forth, contributes what it can give, and then fades forever beyond reach. Self then, is part of this movement, a part through which all men must pass, and the only aspect of the movement for which man alone is responsible. But just as everything must change, the self too eventually disintegrates and dissolves into nothingness. The only thing we know that never changes or passes away is the movement Itself.

As I see it, a contemplative is one who is aware of this movement. At first he strives to go with it, but later, discovering he is being moved without effort, he abandons himself to become part of it—one with it—until finally, he realizes he has never been anything other than this movement Itself.

Conclusion

Although the library, bookstores, and other sources of inquiry yielded no enlightenment, I was not destined to make this journey alone. As it happened, after searching far and wide, I returned home to find help in my own backyard when I discovered that Lucille, my friend and neighbor, was also making this passage. Initially I had been attracted to Lucille because I regarded her as a woman of extraordinary intelligence whose dignity, strength of character, and thoughtfulness of others, spoke to me of the completed individual. Yet it wasn't until this journey that we truly found one another and, like two wanderers in the unknown, the encounter was a mutual surprise, an unexpected bonus which we interpreted as no mere coincidence.

On my way to the library one afternoon, I stopped by Lucille's house to see if she might be taking her daily walk in my direction. While getting her things together she casually asked, "So what's new?" I replied, "I don't have a self anymore." She turned to me with a bemused smile, "You, of all people! No self?" and broke into such hearty laughter that I had to steady her on her feet. When she stopped laughing she asked, "Now tell me, seriously, what does this mean—you have no self?" I told her I didn't know, which was why I was on my way to the library—to find out. Then she began laughing all over again, and her laughter was infectious; after all, what could be more absurd than losing your self?

As we walked along I told her about this unusual state and described some of its effects. At one point she stopped walking and turned to me, "You know," she said, "I recognize what you are describing, but I'm wondering how you know all this, because you are too young. What you are talking about is the aging process, a change of consciousness that is reserved for the final years. It is the last stage in life, a getting ready for a new existence—and you're too young!"

Since Lucille was eighty-five at the time, she was bewildered and a bit skeptical to find her experiences mirrored in a woman almost forty years younger. She couldn't understand how this could be and, naturally, I didn't understand it myself. Nevertheless I suggested that since no one knew the time or hour of death, I might pass away before she did; in which case, I had better be as equally prepared. "Anything is possible, but it's not usual," she replied; then added with motherly concern, "anyway, you're not going to die!" With that, we linked arms tightly and went on our way.

In the next two years of sharing this journey, we were repeatedly struck by the similarity of our experiences, by our individual but similar descriptions, and even by the similarity of the coping mechanisms we had devised in the process—she was continually giving me lessons on how to remember I was forgetful. She told me of her "compensations"—as she called the seeing of "That" which I called Oneness—and of the times she too, had "turned away" because of its overwhelming intensity. In the Passageway, where I felt myself to be walking on the brink of insanity, she thought of herself as walking on the "verge of senility." And where I felt my mind to be in a vise, she described it as a "caul"—a word I had never heard before. Since it would be impossible to recount all of her experiences, let it suffice to say that almost step by step, what I have described of this journey belongs equally to Lucille.

If there was any noticeable difference, it was that her "self," as she told me, had gradually fallen away over a period of years; it had not fallen away abruptly, as in my case. Also, our major concern or emphasis was different. From beginning to end, my concern was the mystery of what remained in the absence of self; whereas for Lucille, the mystery lay in just how much of her self she could live without. She never doubted for a moment, however, that when everything was gone, when everything had been "shed," God would be all that remained—but then, according to her, life would be over. Although my view was not quite the same, the truth is, neither of us had any answers; yet we shared our unknowing, and this sharing was exciting and, at times, indescribably beautiful for we were convinced we were sharing the greatest, most important event of the human experience. Neither birth nor any experience up to this time could hold a candle to the utter reality and awesomeness of this final journey. In truth, this is where life begins!

Three years from the commencement of this journey and at this writing, Lucille, with her faculties and sense of humor intact, passed into the fullness of the new life she had discovered in this transition. Meeting her as I did at this point in my life was tremendously important because, apart from the joy of her companionship, this meeting forever dispelled any notion I may have had about this being a rare, extraordinary, or even private experience. Lucille was totally convinced this experience reflected a transition that the elderly of every generation had gone through and were going through the world over; thus it was all in the natural course of things. That I came upon this journey at an earlier age merely attests to the nature of the contemplative life, which is ever a step ahead of our ordinary, natural expectations. In fact, it is this continual running ahead that gives the contemplative life its supernatural flavor, because grace, transforming nature, is a speeding up of the natural processes; it is an advancement like a rush on time.

This explains why the contemplative does not have to wait until middle age—as Jung would have it—before he finds his "true self." This discovery is a by-product of his union with God, which can be reached at any age—even a very young age—wherein the self is completely integrated when it becomes wholly centered in God. So too, the later journey beyond the "true self" does not have to wait for an advanced age; indeed, arriving at this point in mid-life illustrates, if nothing else, that man does not need a self to live by, not at this stage at least, and not forever. In this way, the supernatural exists to work in a short time what nature, so often waylaid and bogged down by irrelevancies, accomplishes over a longer period of time—and in some cases, never accomplishes at all.

Time then, is a way of accounting for the supernatural without placing it outside natural events or without the need to interpret it as something unnatural or out of the ordinary. At the same time, it is well to remember that because the natural and supernatural are equally of God's own time and making, they are on the same continuum, so that, ultimately, no true separation is possible. One way or the other, God is the only one working in us for our advancement as human beings and as creatures of his own doing. Thus, whether we arrive at our final destination early or late is not, in the long run, all that relevant. Nevertheless, most of us would agree: life gets better, the sooner we get it together.

Because of my meeting with Lucille, two views of this present journey became possible. One view is that the complete loss of self and the realization of what remains is a supernatural event that constitutes, for the contemplative, the second major movement of his relentless journey into God. The other is that this journey is the final process of our natural life-span, wherein self-consciousness is gradually relinquished as we come upon "that" which lies beyond all self. But either way, it is a preparation for a new existence, an entry into a new way of knowing or seeing that is truly the greatest of all man's beginnings, and in no way an ending.

But apart from the contemplatives and the elderly who have made this passage, we will always have with us those who defy the necessity of making such a transition. These are the ones who have never known self-consciousness, and therefore have never known what it is *not* to see. I speak now of those who, by birth, accident, or disease, are considered mentally handicapped, and in particular I think of my niece who was born severely retarded. Long ago her mother assured me that little Marge never developed any real sense of self or of the other, and had never developed an affective system such as we know it. Watching her sit contentedly for hours, as if she were an outside observer on the mysterious world of the self-conscious, I used to wonder what she might be seeing and knowing that made it possible for her to stay in such a satisfied, peaceful state of mind. But like others who live in this unselfconscious state—infants, little children, a variety of individuals—she cannot tell us. Without first having had the relative experience of self-consciousness, there is no way to describe or communicate a non-relative seeing and knowing. It seems that wherever this state occurs, it is wrapped in silence; and even when it is communicated—as only the contemplative can do—it is rarely understood. Truly, it defies any form of intellectualization.

Since a large segment of society lives in this unself-conscious condition without being able to communicate it, the contemplative stands in a unique position to make an accounting for those who cannot do so. And in telling us something of this state, there is the revelation of the Creator's goodness, who has given the little ones to see "that" which the contemplative spends his whole life searching for and, literally, would give his eyetooth to see. Such a divine dispensation is no more mysterious than Christ promising heaven to the criminal on the cross—a common criminal who, for all we know, may have spent his entire life deriding God and hating his neighbor.

For those who have eyes to see, there is no place to look where this Goodness is not revealed. This is the unquestioned object—indeed, the very subject—of the contemplative vision. In this way, he makes an accounting of this goodness, not for himself alone, but for those who cannot tell us what they see beyond a self-conscious dimension. To me, the contemplative's sole function in society is to shed light on this dimension beyond self, and to tell us about the crossing over, which is a journey few can talk about, but a journey everyone is ultimately destined to make.

Although the first movement of the journey ends in the revelation of our union or oneness with God, which is an unmistakable transformation in itself, it nevertheless lacks the finality, the definitiveness, and the abruptness of this second movement, wherein the union of two falls away to reveal only the One remaining. Thus the glimpses of a complete loss of self, described by both St. Teresa and St. John of the Cross as merely "transient" (which somehow they did not foresee as a lasting state), become a permanent reality, a reality of yet another step in the Eternal Movement.

The only mystic I know who says something about this step beyond union, beyond self and God, is Meister Eckhart. In one sense, at least, this could be understood as his "breakthrough," his "bursting forth" into the Godhead, his "crashing through to that which is beyond the idea of God and truth, until it (the soul) reaches the *in principio,* the beginning of beginnings, the origin or source of all goodness and truth." (R. B. Blakney, *Meister Eckhart,* Harper & Row, p. 169). Some of the findings that lie beyond these two landmarks—the falling away of the self and Eckhart's breakthrough—have much in common. Though it would be possible to spend the remainder of these pages pointing out certain similarities, I shall content myself with a single quotation from the master:

When I flowed out from God, all things spoke:
God is. But this cannot make me happy, for it
makes me understand that I am a creature. In the
breakthrough, on the other hand, where I stand
free of my own will and of the will of God and of
all his works and of God himself, there I am
above all creatures and am neither God nor creature. Rather, I am what I was and what I shall remain now and forever ... In this breakthrough I
discover that I and God are one. There I am what
I was, and I grow neither smaller nor bigger...
Here, then, God finds no place in people, for people achieve with this poverty what they were in
eternity and will remain forever. (Matthew Fox,
O.P. *Breakthrough*, Meister Eckhart's Creation
Spirituality in New Translation, Image Books, p.
218)

As I read Eckhart, I read of one who has made the
journey and crossed over. Yet, I also understand he was
so outspoken about what he learned beyond the breakthrough that he eventually incurred the censure of the
Church. Apparently a few theologians were wary lest
the common people—to whom he preached—might
take him seriously and believe him when he talked of
man's *essential* oneness with God, since this is, after all,
a theological taboo. Despite this censure, however, it
says much for theology that Eckhart, a theologian, never
saw anything in his teaching contrary to the doctrines of
the Church.[8] On the contrary, he was certain that on an

---

[8] Recently I came upon this quote from Thomas Aquinas: "And thus
the creature in God is the divine essence itself" (*De Potentia*, q. 3, a.
16, ad 24). I do not know if this quote was taken out of context or
not. As I see it, however, as long as we are creatures we are not in

experiential or practical level he had only penetrated the Truth which theology attempts to define. Eckhart picked up, so to speak, where St. Thomas Aquinas left off, when he not only expanded, but became eloquent, in the areas where his Dominican brother had only fallen silent. Together, these two contemporaries have elaborated a contemplative system that ever remains incomplete if studied separately, or if this study is terminated with the more speculative of the two.

It is regrettable that owing to this, the Spanish mystics found it necessary to bring the descriptions of their experiences into conformity solely with the speculative (Thomistic) aspects of the contemplative life. In doing so, the Eckhartian dimension beyond union was lost, and therefore remains unaccounted for in their writings. As said before, the reason for this is that "what" it becomes possible to know beyond the breakthrough is considered theologically improper.

To speak of an "accidental" oneness or union with God is orthodox; but to speak of an "essential" oneness with God—a oneness in God's essence—is considered unorthodox. The problem is not merely one of description or semantics, but rather, one of experience, for with the falling away of the union of two, there remains only the clear identity of the One. It seems that for the Rhineland mystics in particular, the final emphasis was not so much on the Trinitarian distinctions in the Godhead as the Trinity's essential Unity or Oneness. This is reflected in our own journey where union with distinction even-

---

the divine essence; it is only after we have been transformed into Christ that we become one with the divine essence, in which case, we are no longer "creatures". In fact, in the end there is no "we."

tually gives way to a Unity without distinction—the essential Oneness of the Godhead, that is. Thus it is just as imperative to realize the Unity of the Godhead as it is to realize its Triune distinctions.

This latter reality, however, is not recognized in the contemplative experience because it does not harmonize with the theological insistence on the essential and everlasting separation between Creator and creature. The creature's oneness with God must always retain its separateness or distinction, even though in experience, the creature comes upon an "essential" oneness, a partaking not only of God's isness or existence, but of his whatness or essence. Acknowledging an essential separation, however, Etienne Gilson asks the following question:

> What we want to know is simply this: whether, yes or no, we can admit the possibility of a coincidence, even partial, between the human substance and the Divine substance—whether we can admit it to be then in fact realized.

His answer is this:

> If you lower, were it but for an instant and at any point, the barrier set up by the contingence of being between man and God, then you rob the Christian mystic of his God, and you rob him therefore of his mysticism. He can do without any god who is not inaccessible; the sole God Who by nature is inaccessible is also the sole God he can in no wise do without. (Etienne Gilson, "Unitas Spiritus," *Understanding Mysticism*, Edited by R. Woods, O.P. Image Books, pp. 500-501)

This amounts to saying that union depends on separateness, and in this he is correct; but beyond self this separateness no longer exists, and thus he is also correct in saying that identity of substance (essence, as I call it) between man and God robs the mystic of both his God and his mysticism. In truth, then, coming upon this Oneness is the end of all longing and desire for God, for union or for any type of experience, because this Oneness is by its very nature the ending of the contemplative life—which is why it is the beginning of a new life. In a word, God has become eternally accessible.

As I see it, the root of the problem stems from the belated biblical statement (not mentioned in Genesis) that God made all things from nothing, and that the crux of the disagreement between theologian and mystic lies in the interpretation of this nothing. Since absolute nothing is incomprehensible, it falls, like the essence of God, into the realm of the unknown. That this unknown nothing is not God, is the particular insistence of the theologian; that this unknowable nothing turns out to *be* God, is the final realization of the mystic. In other words, what flowed forth from God in the act of creation (or with creation) was some unknowable aspect of Himself. Thus if we were created from nothing it can only mean nothing *knowable* to the mind, which is the truth, since God's essence is intellectually unknowable. Yet, the experiential understanding of how this works is possible once self has fallen away.

The problem, then, is not merely one of biblical interpretation or semantics; more importantly, it is one of experience, for there does indeed exist a theologically defined oneness or union with God; but there also exists an undefinable essential Oneness for which theology has no words. The difference depends on which side of the breakthrough we stand: whether the self remains, or whether it is dead and buried in the Godhead—as Eckhart puts it. Each side represents two different ways of seeing and knowing, which for now, I can do no more to emphasize.

So however we wish to interpret the nothingness or non-being from which we were made, it is difficult to justify any speculation that God did not make us from himself—his will or uncreated energy—or, as the Platonists prefer, his own mind—since this still does not make us God, does not limit God to matter or to this universe, does not do away with creation, contingency, or change anything at all; nor does it conflict with any relevant Christian belief. (If any, only the notion of eternal damnation might be affected, but who needs this? Certainly God doesn't!) The idea that the created is, in its deepest essence, eternally separated from God, is an idea that no contemplative or mystic could buy into. Instead, they see it much the same as the Evangelist who said, "all we know is that when it (our ultimate destiny) is revealed, we shall be like him"—like Christ. So however it is for Christ in the Godhead, so shall it be for us.

My interest in all this should not be difficult to understand. From the outset of this present journey, I knew I had gone beyond the limits of the particular contemplative frame of reference outlined by the Spanish mystics—who were the major references for my journey and experiences. But I went on to find in Eckhart indications of a lost dimension beyond union and self. Initially I had but a single book on the Master, but at the end of the journey my friend, Father L, passed on to me a list of sources and a number of articles on the mystic and his theology.[9] It seems that the areas where theology is most wont to reinterpret and correct the mystic, are the areas of this lost dimension beyond self. It is because Eckhart is most outspoken here, where theology is most sensitive, that he is unique among the Christian mystics. Thus, where some are wont to draw the line on Eckhart—to keep him in line or from going over the line—is the very point where he breaks through. To keep him this side of the line means to lose this dimension beyond self and thus to cut short the contemplative journey for those who would follow.

In closing this account, I feel a beginning has been made by clearing the ground for much more that remains to be said. As stated initially, this writing stems from the failure to find this movement beyond self in the classical contemplative literature, and though I am no longer concerned for myself, I am concerned for those who may come to a similar end when they discover that their traditional path has suddenly disappeared. Having made this journey I now see clearly, that a dimension unmistakably exists beyond anything that could be described as the self's union with God—be it called spiritual marriage, transforming union, or whatever the terminology one may care to use. For the contemplative to regard such a union as the final or ultimate consumma-

---

[9] In going over the list of his unorthodox statements, while finding some of them to be absurd and false, I found at least half to be true to experience, or true to what is learned by way of experience. It cannot be emphasized enough that the sole value of experience is not experience itself, but rather, what is learned in or through experience—the Truth, in other words. Experiences do not last, they are not eternal; only Truth lasts and is eternal.

tion of his spiritual life is a grave mistake. He is setting his sight at a midway point which, I now see, is too low, too close-in, and too narrow. At this point he may even be so centered in God that he is still subject to the illusion of self's deification, wherein his only feat is to unwittingly shortchange God. Whenever possible, it is best to get beyond such a point, even when letting go means surrendering this union with all its experiences and ensuing qualities of strength, love, certitude, and much more; for as long as there is any feeling, knowledge, or inkling that any self remains, be it a divine self, true self, or even an empirical self, we have not gone far enough.

Of our own accord we cannot cross the line into the unknown, only God knows if we are ready for such a step, only he can take us across and see us through. In fact, self never crosses the line, it simply ceases to be; for if the truth be known, only Christ dies and only Christ rises. Though we may never fully understand this mystery, it is vitally important to realize that such a step exists, that others have taken it, and to be prepared so there will be no illusions about what lies beyond self. For us to give our self to God is, as Eckhart says, to give Him absolutely nothing; but for God to take the self, is for Him to take absolutely everything. Though John of the Cross stresses the giving over the taking, and Meister Eckhart stresses the taking over the giving, the fact remains that no matter how we evaluate this exchange, these are two different movements, two different contemplative experiences. Where the first movement of our life culminates in the union of self and God, the second movement culminates in no union—no self, and no God for that self. The reason for this is that in order to come upon God as he is in Himself—and not as he is in our self—there must be no self. There is no other way.

While reading this account, a friend made the rather droll remark, "It sounds to me like you lost your soul!" Now I had never thought of it this way, yet I liked the idea because I always regarded the soul as God's habitat, a kingdom in which God and self dwell as an unbeatable team; thus, to lose this soul, what could possibly be left? Certainly it would not be me—or you. So what does it mean to lose your soul? I think it means the death of God and self (the unitive state), a descent into hell, and a resurrection on the third day. In heaven we do not speak of souls, we only speak of saints, thus there may be no souls in heaven; I don't know. But if to be a saint in the next life means losing your soul in this life, then it follows that we should all lose our souls. But isn't this what Christ would have us do—to lose our very life (our souls) that we might have eternal life? In new translation this saying turns into: "He who seeks only himself brings himself to ruin, whereas he who brings himself to naught for me discovers who he is." Mt. 10, 39. To this I would add that in coming to nought he will not only discover who he is, but "what" he is, for in God these cannot be separated. *That* he is, *what* he is, *who* he is, *where* he is, in God these are One, and outside this One, nothing is.